2
3.85

W9-CJN-831

BLAKE AND MODERN THOUGHT

Tharmas reared up his hand and stood on the affrighted Ocean

(Vala, f. 22, verso)

BLAKE

&

MODERN THOUGHT

By

DENIS SAURAT

*With eight collotype
plates*

New York

RUSSELL & RUSSELL

1964

FIRST PUBLISHED IN 1929
REISSUED, 1964, BY RUSSELL & RUSSELL, INC.
BY ARRANGEMENT WITH CONSTABLE & CO., LTD. LONDON
L. C. CATALOG CARD NO: 64—18602

PRINTED IN THE UNITED STATES OF AMERICA

TO

E. S.

WHO LOVES BLAKE, BUT REFUSES TO
UNDERSTAND HIM—A TYPICALLY
BLAKEAN ATTITUDE

THE substance of this book has been given as the Foundation Lectures for 1928-1929 in University College, Southampton, although the book was written previously.

————

The author's warm acknowledgments are due to Mr. Laurence Binyon for help generously given in choosing the illustrations from Blake's engravings and pictures.

King's College, London

CONTENTS

CONTENTS

LIST OF ILLUSTRATIONS

INTRODUCTION

FROM the point of view of this study, the essential trait of eighteenth century thought is the shifting of creative power from God to Man. The seventeenth century had still lived on the idea of an absolute creative God, the maker of man, of the world, of the moral law. The eighteenth century began the destructive criticism of that conception of God. It rebelled against the Old Testament presentation of God and of morality. It insisted on the rights of the individual : *les droits de l'homme* and proclaimed the sacredness of the instincts of the natural man. It rebelled against law, and against the abstract intellect that had, they said, been the maker of laws. Voltaire led the rebellion against the ancient conception of God. Rousseau led the fight in favour of the natural man and against law, society, civilisation and intellect. Diderot went further than either, into practical atheism and amoralism. Hume ruined the claims of the abstract intellect. This revolt against an absolute God and an absolute moral law is the essence of liberalism— essentially a negative movement.

[ix]

With the affirmation of the rights of the individual, of the sacredness of natural instincts, came nationalism: individualism among the nations. Races which had so far striven to prove themselves to be offshoots from the peoples of the Bible began to reverse the process, and began to try and prove themselves the origin of mankind or of civilisation and to imagine how the peoples of the Bible might have descended from Celtic or Germanic ancestors. Here we see the beginnings of a constructive process in the conception of history and of the world.

But the complete change came with the positive phase when man, having deplaced God from the throne of the Creator, tried to hoist himself into that Supreme Seat. This was to lead to the idealism of the nineteenth century: the doctrine that it was the mind of man that created the world. But the German philosophers from Kant to Hegel only codified eighteenth century thought. Men vastly inferior to them in logical power, but perhaps superior in intuitive and psychological insight, like Swedenborg and de Saint Martin, had preceded them in the identification of the powers of man and the powers of God. Diderot himself had had the

[x]

intuition that the creative forces were in man and in nature. When the German philosophers came, the change in men's mentality had been made. They brought a tremendous technical apparatus—now largely felt to be antiquated like ancient machinery—to the intellectualisation of a change in *feeling*; and that change in feeling had been expressed already by the eighteenth century *philosophes*. So that after all this much ridiculed appellation was justified: they had not had the technique of philosophy, but they had had the ideas. And now that the technical machinery is largely superannuated, we turn to the eighteenth century *philosophes* as to the heralds of the change that was to make modern thought.

For the difference between us and the people of old in our own race lies, whether for good or evil, in this change of mentality. We may call it intellectual democracy: not only have we claimed our share in the government of the world, but we have claimed our share in the making of it. From Kant and his distinction between phenomena and noumena to Einstein and relativity, modern thought has gone this way.

Blake stands at the moment of the change.

[xi]

He has given it perhaps its most forcible expression:

> Thou also dwellest in eternity.
> Thou art a man, God is no more.
> Thy own humanity learn to adore,
> For that is the Spirit of life.

Perhaps we have learnt only too much our own divinity to adore, and a little criticism of how we came by the notion might do us good. We shall therefore find in Blake the typical notions of his time:

Liberalism: the rebellion against the God of the Old Testament, against the moral law, against the abstract intellect;

Nationalism: the idealisation of our own race to an entirely extravagant extent;

Idealism: replacing God by Man as a Creator, or identifying Man with God.

Now we were not the first races to come to these conceptions. Therefore a most curious characteristic of this movement is the search for help in the past. Modern man, treading on what seemed to him new and dangerous ground, was glad to find the traces of men who had gone before over the same quagmires and deserts. Hence the eighteenth century craze

for all manner of quaint learning, ancient
tradition, exotic faiths. Help was wanted.
Help was found.

The Gnostics had rebelled before against
Jehovah and his laws; and the Manicheans
and Albigenses and the popular pantheism of
the late middle ages had culminated in a first
outburst at the Renaissance. The classical
temper of the seventeenth century had for a
time reacted against this, but now all those
threads were gathered up again. Blake is full
of gnostic lore.

The Jewish Cabalists had worked out the
identification of God and Man to its furthest
possible limits; and a long string of Christian
Cabalists from Pico della Mirandola to Fludd
and Swedenborg, had taught the European
mind that in the Cabala there was a living
spring of fertilising ideas. Blake is full of the
Cabala and of its Christian exponents.

Hindoo philosophy and mythology was being
discovered and the discoverers read their own
meanings into it. Blake knew of India and
derived inspiration from its chaotic cosmo-
gonies. Also the science of the time was turning
its attention to the remote past of our races, and
the first theories of the antiquarians as to the

part played in the past by the Celts were in full harmony with the national aspirations of Western European peoples.

Mingling therefore with the great modern movements of liberalism, nationalism, idealism, we shall, at every turn, find in Blake a reversion to old lore, gnostic or cabalistic or occultist of every kind, also a rummaging among pseudo-scientific theories on the origin of races and crude knowledge of Indian religion.

But the two tendencies, the modern and the occultist-exotic, are the same: the modern mind, awakening to clearer conceptions of its wishes, was merely looking for outside help wherever help could be found.

Thus Blake is a curious witness of his own time; and as his time was merely the dawn of ours, he is a curious and important *witness of our own mentality*.

 I have tried as much as I could to let Blake tell his own tale. When it was not to be understood, I have called in witnesses as nearly as possible of his own time. It has been my aim to bring in as little as I could of my own interpretation— since Blake suffers very greatly from an excess of interpretation.

*   *   *   *   *   *

It is not my intention here to demonstrate that Voltaire, Rousseau, Diderot, Hume and their contemporaries rebelled against the old conceptions of God, Morality, Intellect, Society: that would be to bring the whole intellectual history of the century into this book. I shall therefore take it for granted that Blake was a man of his time and knew Voltaire and Rousseau. I am concerned here with Blake specifically; and I am bringing, not a complete explanation of Blake's thought or myths (this will no doubt take several generations of scholars)—but *a contribution to the study* of Blake. These are the points I have tried to make clear. I am fully aware that many points remain obscure and make no claim to any sort of completeness, even in the subjects I have tackled.

May I state my faith that in due time, after long perseverance and granted a certain amount of luck, scholarship will explain Blake? I have tried only to make a beginning and, perhaps through personal taste, have concerned myself chiefly here

With fantasies of his peculiar thought.

PART I

LIBERALISM: THE REBELLION AGAINST DOGMA, MORALITY, REASON

I. BLAKE & THE GNOSTICS

NATURALLY, Blake being a deeply religious man, the rebellion against God which characterised his century took a religious turn with him. He was really in sympathy with Voltaire's onslaught and at the same time profoundly shocked by what was, to him, Voltaire's irreligious spirit. This synthesis of rebellion with religion had already been achieved by the Gnostics. Blake therefore found himself in deep and fairly complete sympathy with them. He had easy access to their doctrines: Mosheim had published in Latin in 1753 his *Commentaries on the affairs of the Christians before the time of Constantine the Great*, in which the gnostic tenets are very fully explained. Blake could read Latin. I shall not attempt to prove that Blake knew that book, or any of the books to be drawn upon later in this study. The fact seems to me of little importance. Blake may or may not have read Mosheim, Edward Williams, Rosenroth, Sonnerat, who will be my chief witnesses. But Blake frequented

Swedenborgian circles where such books were the subject of perpetual discussion. Blake's highly individual temperament in any case gave a strong personal twist to whatever he read or heard. Thus I will content myself with showing that certain conceptions are present, and in the possession of the public, in the eighteenth century before Blake and that they are present also in Blake's work. We deal here in currents of thought and not in plagiarism or imitation. In some cases, Blake, from general sympathy, no doubt reconstructed ideas or myths which existed before him and round him and which he had not heard of. He was thereby expressing his own personality as a man of his time, and also as a man of genius who can see on the slightest hint the fullest implications of an idea.

Let me add, perhaps a little fancifully, that Blake, in taking to gnostic lore, was behaving typically as a man of the lower classes in Western Europe. The Church, and the Churches, have never quite succeeded in eradicating from the masses in the West certain heresies or ways of thinking and behaving that are historically connected with gnosticism and Manicheism. The great outburst of the Albi-

[4]

genses in the thirteenth century was a counter offensive against the Church and traces of it remained till the Reformation, a movement which gave a new life to many heretical conceptions. The English sects of the seventeenth century frequently voiced popular religious ideas that had been repressed by catholicism. A vein of popular pantheism runs through the Middle Ages into modern times[1] and survivals of gnostic and Manichean tenets are carried along with it. The Jewish Cabala has historical association with such ideas; it is often called, with good reason, Jewish gnosticism; but we get sight of it in history for the first time with the school of Isaac the Blind, and that was in Provence, just before the semi-Manichean explosion of the Albigenses. So that the brilliant but short lived Provençal civilisation was connected—in what precise manner we have yet to study—with both gnosticism and the Cabala. The onslaught of the Northern barons crushed Provence under Simon de Montfort; but the ideas were not killed. They lingered on in the lower classes and found occasional

[1]It has been studied by Jundt in his *Histoire du panthéisme populaire au moyen âge et au XVIᵉ siècle*. Strasbourg, Paris. 1875, a book now to be rewritten by the light of recent historical research. Napoleon Peyrat in his *Histoire des Albigeois* also gives invaluable information.

[5]

expression. Victor Hugo's very strange metaphysics, for instance, are such an expression of
what has remained in the religious mind of the
people of Western Europe even as late as the
nineteenth century.

It is not strange, therefore, to find Blake, a
man of the people, swayed by gnostic ideas;
he was obeying impulses similar to those which
had urged into heresy on many occasions the
races to which he belonged, as the Lollards,
did we know them better, would probably tell.
In Mosheim, we find every element that was
to go to the making of Blake's conception of
Urizen, the God of this world. The Gnostics are
described as "pretending that they were able to
communicate to mankind, at present held in
bondage by the Architect of the World, a correct
knowledge of the true and ever living God."[1]
This is a very apt description of what Blake
himself thought of his own mission. And here is
the general statement which covers the very
centre of the mythology of the whole of Blake's
prophetic books.

"That the world and all terrestrial bodies were not
the work of the Supreme Being, but were formed out

[1]Mosheim, *Commentaries*, vol. i. pp. 303-305. I quote from the English
translation by R. S. Vidal, London, 1813.

of matter by a nature either evil in its origin, or that had fallen into a state of depravity and that the whole race of mankind instead of worshipping the Father of Light and Life, universally paid their homage to the Founder and Prince of this nether world."[1]

Saturninus held similarly that

"in addition to the Deity, of whom no one had any knowledge, there existed from all eternity a material principle intrinsically evil and corrupt, over which presided a certain governor or prince."[2]

We shall find again this *Deity of whom no one had any knowledge* when we consider the constructive part of Blake's system. The cosmogony of the Gnostics has largely inspired Blake, as we shall then see, but for the present I wish to draw attention first of all only to this rebellious spirit in him, the most evident trait of the century, and to show how gnostic criticism helped him.

For the Gnostics, Jewish law had been "promulgated by the architect or founder of this world and Christ had come to abrogate the Jewish law,"[3] and to save mankind from the false God.

[1]Mosheim, i. 310   [2]Mosheim, ii. 211, 212.
[3]Mosheim, i. 310, 313, 288, 293 (on Valentine).

[7]

This Demiurgus was so "puffed up with arrogance and pride as to imagine that he himself was the only God and in consequence thereof to arrogate to himself . . . the honours due to the Supreme Deity."[1]

This is one of the chief traits of Urizen, who becomes thus for Blake the father of all religious superstition as well as of law.

Marcion had drawn a distinction between two Gods: the Good One and the Just One. The Good One had created the invisible world. The Just One, who was warlike and cruel, had created the visible world. He was the author of Mosaic revelation. He was not entirely bad, being just, but "he took vengeance on all those who neglected his laws."[2]

In the same spirit as Mosheim's Marcion, Blake looked upon "vengeance" as the abomination of desolation, and on justice as a mere form of vengeance. "Mutual forgiveness of each vice" was his gospel, as it was, later, to be that of Victor Hugo, for similar reasons, both historical and personal.

Also Blake's Urizen was not entirely bad, as we shall abundantly see.

Marcion's Just God also gave rewards—and

[1]Mosheim, i. 288.   [2]Mosheim, i. 322 to 325.

both things, punishment and rewards, were held unworthy of the Supreme God. This led to a conception of Jesus, which is Blake's conception in *the Everlasting Gospel*. The Just God perceived that no respect whatever was paid by Jesus to his law, and therefore became Jesus' greatest enemy.[1]

The general conception of the mythological figure of Urizen is thus found in the Gnostics.

Urizen is the Creator of this world, and he is a bad creator: he has done his work in evil fashion; matter and this cosmos are evil things. Urizen is the legislator of this world, and therefore his laws are bad; the rules taught by Moses are bad; the moral rules prevailing in our society are bad.

Urizen is a deceiver; he has taught the world lies so that the world should worship him. He is the father of all superstition; all dogmas promulgated by established religions are lies.

This rebellion of Blake against dogma and morality, this reversal of all values, is the essential aspect of his creed. Here he speaks with no uncertain voice. We shall find him fanciful and extravagant in his theories of the supremacy of the English. We shall find him

[1]Mosheim, i. 325-329.

[9]

complicated to the verge of madness in his occultist idealism; but on the question of dogma and morality he is clear, simple, forcible and often profound. His rebellion against the moral law is the one unmistakable attitude he is persistent in. We shall see him falter in his attack against dogma; he speaks out unhesitatingly against the orthodox ideas of morality.

II. THE ATTACK AGAINST THE
GOD OF THIS WORLD

BLAKE is the inheritor of all the jeers against religion and the orthodox conception of God which had accumulated from the *libertins* to Voltaire and his successors. This is how he mimics official religion in his version of the Lord's prayer according to this world:

Doctor Thornton's Tory Translation, translated out of its disguise in the Classical and Scotch languages into the vulgar English.
Our Father Augustus Caesar, who art in these thy substantial Astronomical Telescopic Heavens, Holiness to thy Name or Title, and reverence to thy Shadow. Thy Kingship come upon Earth first and then in Heaven. Give us day by day our Real Taxed Substantial Money bought Bread; deliver from the Holy Ghost whatever cannot be Taxed; for all is debts and Taxes between Caesar and us and one another; lead us not to read the Bible, but let our Bible be Virgil and Shakespeare; and deliver us from Poverty in Jesus, that Evil One. For thine is the Kingship (or) Allegoric Godship, and the Power,

[11]

or War, and the Glory, or an Allegory of Kings and nothing else.

AMEN.

The Marriage of Heaven and Hell teaches us that we have been deceived and that the Bible has been written by the wrong side:

"for this history has been adopted by both parties," and Blake intends to give us the *Bible of Hell*, and to teach us to read even our Bible *in its infernal or diabolical sense.*[1]

In his notes on Watson's apology, Blake takes up the expression "the word of God" and adds:

They seem to Forget that there is a God of this World, A God Worship'd in this World as God and set above all that is call'd God.

But Blake, of course, cannot think of atheism. He is, therefore, driven to the gnostic theory that the God of this World was himself a rebel against the Real God; or at least an inferior and mistaken God. *"Thinking as I do that the Creator of this world is a very cruel being,"* says Blake in sober prose.[2]

[1] Keynes, 1 vol. edition, pp. 192-202; all my references shall be to that edition.
[2] Vision of the last Judgment, p. 844.

[12]

Urizen is a rebel:

"What night he led the starry hosts thro' the wide
    wilderness"[1]
In that dread night when Urizen call'd the stars
    round his feet;
Then burst the center from its orb, and found a
    place beneath;
And Earth conglob'd, in narrow room, roll'd its
    sulphur Sun.[1]

Even as Milton's Satan conferring with his
lieutenant, we see Urizen, Prince of Light,
confer with Luvah[2]:

" 'Thou Luvah,' said the Prince of Light, 'behold
    our sons and daughters
Reposed on beds; let them sleep on; do thou alone
    depart
Into thy wished Kingdom, wherein Majesty and Power
We may erect a throne; deep in the North I place
    my lot, . . .'

" Urizen cast deep darkness round him, silent
    brooding death,
Eternal death to Luvah; raging, Luvah pour'd
The Lances of Urizen from chariots round the holy
    tent,
Discord began, and yells and cries shook the wide
    firmament."

[1]Pp. 220, 228-229.   [2]Pp. 298 to 302.

" 'But Urizen, with darkness overspreading all the
armies,
Sent round his heralds secretly commanding to depart
Into the north. Sudden with thunder's sound his
multitudes
Retreat from the fierce conflict, all the sons of Urizen
at once
Must'ring together in thick clouds, leaving the rage
of Luvah
To pour its fury on himself and on the Eternal
Man.' "

We shall come back to the complications of
these happenings when we study Blake's cosmogony. I wish here only to insist on this
rebellious character of Urizen, which makes
rebellion against him a duty.

This rebel against the true God is the Creator
of the world. The whole *first Book of Urizen* is
devoted to a description of his labours. But
again and again we are told in detail (not
always coherent detail) how this creation took
place and its fatal character is insisted upon:

Eternity groan'd and was troubled at the Image of
Eternal Death.
The Wandering Man bow'd his faint head and
Urizen descended—
And *the one must have murder'd the Man if he had not
descended*—

[14]

Indignant, muttering low thunders, Urizen descended,
Gloomy sounding: "Now I am God from Eternity
   to Eternity."[1]

Urizen claims the supreme title:

"Am I not God?" said Urizen. "Who is Equal to me?
Do I not stretch the heavens abroad, or fold them up
   like a garment?"
He spoke, mustering his heavy clouds around him,
   black, opake.
Then thunders roll'd around and lightnings darted
   to and fro;
His visage chang'd to darkness, and his strong right
   hand came forth
To cast Ahania to the Earth. . . ."[2]

We shall find later that all this meets the idea
that the Creation is really a Fall, a limitation,
a contraction of the true God: an idea which is
partly found in gnosticism and fully expressed
in the Cabala.
The chief aspect here of Urizen is that of the
law giver[3]:

   "Adam stood in the garden of Eden
   And Noah on the mountains of Ararat;

[1]P. 290, cf. 302; this strange line: *the one would have murder'd the man* . . .
will be explained in Part III.
[2]P. 324.   [3]Pp. 273, 256, 257

[15]

They saw Urizen give his Laws to the Nations
By the hands of the children of Los.''

   .   .   .   .

"He in darkness clos'd view'd all his race,
And his soul sicken'd! he curs'd
Both sons and daughters; for he saw
That no flesh nor spirit could keep
His iron laws one moment.''

   .   .   .   .

"Cold he wander'd on high, over their cities
In weeping and pain and woe;
And wherever he wander'd, in sorrows
Upon the aged heavens,
A cold shadow follow'd behind him
Like a spider's web, moist, cold and dim,
Drawing out from his sorrowing soul,
The dungeon-like heaven dividing,
Where ever the footsteps of Urizen
Walked over the cities in sorrow;
Till a Web, dark and cold, throughout all
The tormented element stretch'd
From the sorrows of Urizen's soul.
And the Web is a Female in embrio.
None could break the Web, no wings of fire,

So twisted the cords, and so knotted
The meshes, twisted like to the human brain.

And all call'd it the Net of Religion.

[16]

III. THE ATTACK AGAINST THE MORAL LAW

THE moral law being the law given us by this false god (and we shall see later that this false god, Urizen, is the Intellect) the moral law is necessarily evil. It is our duty to rebel against it. As the Gnostics pointed out, Christ has given us an example of this rebellion. Hence *The Everlasting Gospel.*

> Was Jesus gentle? . . .
> Was Jesus humble? . . .
> Was Jesus chaste? . . .
> He mocked the Sabbath and he mock'd
> The Sabbath's God. . . .

Hence the *Marriage of Heaven and Hell.*

"If Jesus Christ is the greatest man, you ought to love him in the greatest degree; now hear how he has given his sanction to the law of ten commandments: did he not mock at the sabbath, and so the sabbath's God? murder those who were murder'd because of him? turn away the law from the woman taken in adultery? steal the labor of others to support him? bear false witness when he omitted making a

defence before Pilate? covet when he pray'd for his
disciples, and when he bid them shake off the dust
of their feet against such as refused to lodge them?
I tell you, no virtue can exist without breaking these
ten commandments. Jesus was all virtue, and acted
from impulse, not from rules."[1]

This is how morality is stigmatised:

"O Polypus of Death! O Spectre over Europe and
    Asia,
Withering the Human Form by Laws of Sacrifice
    for Sin!
By Laws of Chastity and Abhorrence I am wither'd up:
Striving to create a Heaven in which all shall be
    pure and holy
In their Own Selfhoods: in Natural Selfish Chastity
    to banish Pity
And dear Mutual Forgiveness, and to become One
    Great Satan
Inslav'd to the most powerful Selfhood: to murder
    the Divine Humanity
In whose sight all are as the dust and who chargeth
    his Angels with folly!
Ah! weak and wide astray! Ah! shut in narrow
    doleful form!
Creeping in reptile flesh upon the bosom of the
    ground!"[2]

[1]Cf. pp. 753, 764, 767, 770, 833 on Caiaphas and Pilate, 839, 842,
1028: if morality was Christianity, Socrates was the Saviour.
[2]P. 643, cf. 714: Compell'd into a shape of moral virtue against the
Lamb.

Not only the mosaic virtues, but the platonic virtues are banned:

"Then Los conducts the Spirits to be Vegetated into
Great Golgonooza, free from the four iron pillars of
    Satan's Throne,
(Temperance, Prudence, Justice, Fortitude, the
    four pillars of tyranny)
That Satan's Watch-Fiends touch them not before
    they Vegetate."[1]

Blake comes thus to the general statement: Will is always evil.[2]
This is borne out by a general theory as to good and evil which is the basis of the *Marriage of Heaven and Hell*:

"Without Contraries is no progression. Attraction and Repulsion, Reason and Energy, Love and Hate, are necessary to Human existence. From these contraries spring what the religious call Good and Evil. Good is the passive that obeys Reason. Evil is the active springing from Energy.
Good is Heaven. Evil is Hell.

THE VOICE OF THE DEVIL

All Bibles or sacred codes have been the causes of the following errors:

1. That Man has two real existing principles: Viz. a Body and a Soul.

[1]P. 523.   [2]P. 933.

2. That Energy, call'd Evil, is alone from the Body; and that Reason, call'd Good, is alone from the Soul.
3. That God will torment Man in Eternity for following his Energies.
But the following Contraries to these are True:
1. Man has no Body distinct from his Soul; for that call'd Body is a portion of Soul discern'd by the five Senses, the chief inlets of Soul in this age.
2. Energy is the only life, and is from the Body; and Reason is the bound or outward circumference of Energy.
3. Energy is Eternal Delight."[1]

Justice as mankind understands it is necessarily evil. Man has no more right than God to "torment Man for following his energies." Justice is mere vengeance, and all virtue is forgiveness: the *punisher's* state is eternal death.[2]

"And the appearance of a Man was seen in the
   Furnaces
Saving those who have sinned from the punishment
   of the Law
(In pity of the punisher whose state is eternal death)
And keeping them from Sin by the mild counsels of
   his love";[2]

But the One virtue against which Blake is most persistent is chastity; and consequently

[1]P. 191.   [2]P. 616.

[20]

jealousy is to him an unbearable thing and the
source of untold woe. This is connected in his
mind with several theories.

In the century, too, the rebellion against the
moral law very largely means rebellion against
the accepted rules of sexual morality. Writers
enlarge against morality in general when they
mean sexual morality. It is difficult to vindicate
the right to murder or to steal; but to find
arguments in favour of a frequent change of
wives or mistresses is a pleasanter and less dangerous task. Diderot in his *Supplement au voyage de
Bougainville* gives us the keynote of this kind of
thinking, for which Rousseau's return to Nature
had been a preparation and the amiable laxity
of Voltaire's tales a pleasant illustration.

Blake reinforces these theories. He points out
that enjoyment and not abstinence is the
source of life.

> "Abstinence sows sand all over
> The ruddy limbs and flaming hair,
> But Desire Gratified
> Plants fruits of life and beauty there.
>
> In a wife I would desire
> What in whores is always found—
> The lineaments of Gratified desire."[1]

[1]P. 99

And the *Proverbs of Hell* are very edifying:

"Joys impregnate Sorrows bring forth.
The soul of sweet delight can never be defiled.
Exuberance is beauty.
Sooner murder an infant in its cradle than nurse
　　unacted desires."

Even ideas spring from desire:

"Enjoyment and not abstinence is the food of the
　　intellect."

"Those who restrain desire do so because theirs is
weak enough to be restrained; and the restrainer
or reason usurps its place and governs the unwilling.
And being restrain'd, it by degrees becomes passive,
till it is only the shadow of desire."[1]

Desire is essentially sexual desire:

"And many of the Eternal Ones laughed after their
　　manner:

'Have you known the Judgment that is arisen among
　　the
Zoas of Albion, where a Man dare hardly to embrace
His own Wife for the terrors of Chastity that they call
By the name of Morality? their Daughters govern all
In hidden deceit! they are Vegetable, only fit for
　　burning.
Art and Science cannot exist but by Naked Beauty
　　display'd.'
　　　　　　　　　　　[1]P. 1036 and pp. 191-3.
　　　　　　　　　　　[22]

Then those in Great Eternity who contemplate on
    Death
Said thus: 'What seems to Be, Is, To those to whom
It seems to Be, and is productive of the most dreadful
Consequences to those to whom it seems to Be, even
    of
Torments, Despair, Eternal Death.' "[1]

Jealousy is consequently a great evil. The
whole wonderful poem of the *Visions of the
Daughters of Albion* is written against it, and some
parts are worthy—in thought—of modern
psycho-analysts (being in expression far above
their power).

"With cold floods of abstraction, and with forests of
    solitude,
To build him castles and high spires, where kings
    and priests may dwell;
Till she who burns with youth, and knows no fixed
    lot, is bound
In spells of law to one she loaths? and must she drag
    the chain
Of life in weary lust? must chilling, murderous
    thoughts obscure
The clear heaven of her eternal spring; to bear the
    wintry rage
Of a harsh terror, driv'n to madness, bound to hold
    a rod

[1]P. 618.

[23]

Over her shrinking shoulders all the day, and all the
night
To turn the wheel of false desire, and longings that
wake her womb
To the abhorred birth of cherubs in the human
form,
That live a pestilence and die a meteor, and are no
more;
Till the child dwell with one he hates, and do the
deed he loaths,
And the impure scourge force his seed into its unripe
birth
Ere yet his eyelids can behold the arrows of the
day?"[1]

. . . .

"The moment of desire! the moment of desire! The
virgin
That pines for man shall awaken her womb to
enormous joys
In the secret shadows of her chamber: the youth
shut up from
The lustful joy shall forget to generate and create an
amorous image
In the shadows of his curtains and in the folds of his
silent pillow.
Are not these the places of religion, the rewards of
continence,
The self enjoyings of self denial? why dost thou seek
religion?

[1]P. 211.

[24]

Is it because acts are not lovely that thou seekest
    solitude
Where the horrible darkness is impressed with
    reflections of desire?"[1]

This goes deep with Blake, and is connected
with perhaps the most modern and the most
daring of his theories—which is the most
ancient also, as we shall find later: the theory
that the human personality is a delusion,
that the individual does not exist. States
only exist and states only are to be cultivated
or restrained. And the state of sexual bliss
is to be cultivated whenever and wherever
it can be.[2]

This is the ideal that Oothoon the unfaithful
proposes to her husband:

"But silken nets and traps of adamant will Oothoon
    spread,
And catch for thee girls of mild silver, or of furious
    gold.
I'll lie beside thee on a bank and view their wanton
    play
In lovely copulation, bliss on bliss, with Theotormon:
Red as the rosy morning, lustful as the first born
    beam,

[1]P. 213.
[2]This theory of states is so modern as to be, in fact, Proust's theory
of the moment.

[25]

Oothoon shall view his dear delight, nor e'er with
    jealous cloud
Come in the heaven of generous love, nor selfish
    blightings bring."[1]

Here is the condemnation of the usual law.

    ". . . such is that false
And Generating Love, a pretence of love to destroy
    love,
Cruel hipocrisy, unlike the lovely delusions of Beulah,
And cruel forms, unlike the merciful forms of Beulah's
    Night.

They know not why they love nor wherefore they
    sicken and die,
Calling that Holy Love which is Envy, Revenge and
    Cruelty,
Which separated the stars from the mountains, the
    mountains from Man
And left Man, a little grovelling Root outside of
    Himself."[2]

The cause of the Fall, of the division of the
One Total Being into small separate individuals,
is thus stated to be this evil sort of love.
Thus individuals have been wrongly created.
In the true state of innocence, all men love all
women and have free access to them. Jerusalem
is all women in one, and exists in the state of

[1]P. 214.   [2]P. 580.

Eden; in this world, women are individualised, and that is Vala, *"the Shadow of Jerusalem."*[1]

Thus Blake reverses the usual conception. Sexual love is legitimate when it goes to *all* women; it is wrong when it limits itself to one woman. For Sex, as we shall see later, is a principle of division: Salvation is in reunion:

"Humanity knows not of Sex: wherefore are Sexes
    in Beulah?
In Beulah the Female lets down her beautiful
    Tabernacle
Which the Male enters magnificent between her
    Cherubim
And becomes One with her, mingling, condensing
    in Self-love
The Rocky Law of Condemnation and double
    Generation and Death."[2]

This sexual distinction is only one case in a category of erroneous distinctions:

"What is a Wife and what is a Harlot? What is a
    Church and What
Is a Theatre? are they two and not One? can they
    Exist Separate?
Are not Religion and Politics the Same Thing?
    Brotherhood is Religion,
O Demonstrations of Reason Dividing Families in
    Cruelty and Pride!"[3]

[1]P. 568.   [2]P. 607.   [3]P. 658.

[27]

Thus is Crabb Robinson's report that Blake believed in a community of women confirmed not only by separate passages in the poems, but by Blake's general metaphysical theories. In theory, Blake believed in promiscuity. His biographers tell us that in practice he was prevented by his wife's tears from introducing even one *handmaiden* into the home.[1]

So he comforted himself with dreams of Beulah:

"And the Divine Voice was heard in the Songs of
    Beulah, saying:

'When I first Married you, I gave you all my whole
    Soul.

I thought that you would love my loves and joy in
    my delights,

Seeking for pleasures in my pleasures, O Daughter
    of Babylon.

Then thou wast lovely, mild and gentle; now thou
    hast cruelly

Cut off my loves in fury till I have no love left for
    thee.

Thy love depends on him thou lovest, and on his
    dear loves

Depend thy pleasures, which thou hast cut off by
    Jealousy.

Therefore I show my Jealousy and set before you
    Death.

[1]Mona Wilson, *Life of Blake*, p. 59.

Behold Milton descended to Redeem the Female
  Shade
From Death Eternal; such your lot, to be continually
  Redeem'd
By death and misery of those you love and by
  Annihilation.
When the Sixfold Female perceives that Milton
  annihilates
Himself, that seeing all his loves by her cut off, he
  leaves
Her also, intirely abstracting himself from Female
  loves,
She shall relent in fear of death; she shall begin to give
Her maidens to her husband, delighting in his
  delight.
And then and then alone begins the happy Female
  joy.' "[1]

But in this world things are not so well arranged;
the solution is therefore, "Mutual forgiveness
of each vice," by which Blake means mutual
acception of each other's sexual frailties:

"When the Druids demanded Chastity from Woman
  and all was lost.

'How can the Female be Chaste, O thou stupid
  Druid,' Cried Los,
Without the Forgiveness of Sins in the merciful
  clouds of Jehovah

[1]P. 530.

[29]

And without the Baptism of Repentance to wash
    away Calumnies and
The Accusations of Sin, that each may be Pure in
    their Neighbours' sight?"[1]

This theory of Jealousy is carried to its maxi-
mum elevation in the third book of Jerusalem.
When Jesus is to be born, Joseph is jealous; but
the sweetness of Mary wins him over, and he
allows Jesus to come. Thus, had jealousy had
its way, mankind could not have been saved.

" 'Ah my Mary!' said Joseph, weeping over and
    embracing her closely in
His arms: 'Doth he forgive Jerusalem, and not
    exact Purity from her who is
Polluted? I heard his voice in my sleep and his
    Angel in my dream,
Saying, Doth Jehovah Forgive a Debt only on con-
    dition that it shall
Be Payed? Doth he Forgive Pollution only on con-
    ditions of Purity?
That Debt is not Forgiven! That Pollution is not
    Forgiven!

[1]Pp. 671-673, cf. in opposition, 688-689: then all the Males con-
joined into one Male: where a terrible caricature of true Unity is
formed and all

> "The Jealousies become Murderous, uniting together in Rahab
> A Religion of Chastity, forming a Commerce to sell Loves,
> With Moral Law an Equal Balance not going down with decision.
> Therefore the Male severe and cruel, fill'd with stern Revenge,
> Mutual Hate returns and mutual Deceit and mutual Fear."

Such is the Forgiveness of the Gods, the Moral
    Virtues of the
Heathen whose tender Mercies are Cruelty. But
    Jehovah's Salvation
Is without Money and without Price, in the continual
    Forgiveness of Sins,
In the Perpetual Mutual Sacrifice in Great Eternity;
    for behold,
There is none that liveth and Sinneth not! And this
    is the Covenant
Of Jehovah: If you Forgive one another, so shall
    Jehovah Forgive You,
That He Himself may Dwell among You. Fear not
    then to take
To thee Mary thy Wife, for she is with Child by the
    Holy Ghost.' "[1]

Thus end in Blake the eighteenth century
theories of the legitimacy of instinct, which had
grown from Rousseau to Diderot, and thus is
glorified *le culte de la sensibilité*.

[1]Pp. 666-667.

IV. THE ATTACK AGAINST
INTELLECT

THIS *culte de la sensibilité* is connected with another great movement of the end of the century: anti-rationalism.[1] It is linked at the same time with the attack on God and with idealism. This world is badly made because it is made by Urizen, and Urizen is Intellect. Man's Intellect constructs the outside world, but constructs it wrongly. This is also an aspect of the Fall.

Now this criticism of the Intellect is arrived at by the Intellect. It is Reason which understands and discounts its own limitations. We shall therefore find in Blake a rationalist as well as an anti-rationalist and in this mixture he belongs peculiarly to his time.

That Blake is a rationalist with his contemporaries has not been sufficiently insisted upon. After all his attacks on Voltaire, he could say to Crabb Robinson that, "he understood the

[1]See on this F. B. Kaye's admirable summary in his *Mandeville* (Clarendon Press), vol. i. p. lxxix sq.

Bible in a spiritual sense. As to the Natural sense, he said Voltaire was commissioned by God to expose that. *'I have had,'* he said, *'much intercourse with Voltaire, and he said to me: I blasphemed the Son of Man and it shall be forgiven me, but they (the enemies of Voltaire) blasphemed the Holy Ghost in me and it shall not be forgiven them.'* "[1]

Blake went as far as Voltaire when the rationalist mood was on him. Here is his explanation of the origin of religions:

"The ancient Poets animated all sensible objects with Gods or Geniuses, calling them by the names and adorning them with the properties of woods, rivers, mountains, lakes, cities, nations, and whatever their enlarged and numerous senses could perceive.

And particularly they studied the genius of each city and country, placing it under its mental deity; Till a system was formed, which some took advantage of, and enslav'd the vulgar by attempting to realize or abstract the mental deities from their objects: thus began Priesthood;

Choosing forms of worship from poetic tales.

And at length they pronounc'd that the Gods had order'd such things.

Thus men forgot that All deities reside in the human breast.

[1]Crabb Robinson, *Diary* (Symions), p. 301.

[33]

A Memorable Fancy

The Prophets Isaiah and Ezekiel dined with me, and I asked them how they dared so roundly to assert that God spoke to them; and whether they did not think at the time that they would be misunderstood, and so be the cause of imposition.
Isaiah answer'd: 'I saw no God, nor heard any, in
    finite organical perception; but my senses discover'd the infinite in everything, and as I was then perswaded, and remain confirm'd that the voice of honest indignation is the voice of God, I cared not for consequences, but wrote.' "[1]

The Voltarian character of this theory of Priesthood (*a system was formed which some took advantage of and enslaved the vulgar*) is apparent enough. Blake can explain the whole of religion allegorically:

The worship of God is: Honouring his gifts in other men, each according to his genius, and loving the greatest men best: those who envy or calumniate great men hate God; for there is no other God."[2]

which is not atheism, but the theory of immanence.
To the end this spirit remained with Blake, since in *Jerusalem*, he says *to the Christians*:

[1]Pp. 195-196.   [2]P. 202.

"I know of no other Christianity and of no other Gospel than the liberty both of body and mind to exercise the Divine Arts of Imagination, Imagination, the real and eternal World of which this Vegetable Mortal Bodies are no more. The Apostles knew of no other Gospel. What were all their spiritual gifts? What is the Divine Spirit? is the Holy Ghost any other than an Intellectual Fountain? What is the Harvest of the Gospel and its Labours? What is that Talent which it is a curse to hide? What are the Treasures of Heaven which we are to lay up for ourselves, are they any other than Mental Studies and Performances? What are all the Gifts of the Gospel, are they not all Mental Gifts? . . . What is the Joy of Heaven but Improvement in the things of the Spirit? What are the Pains of Hell but Ignorance, Bodily Lust, Idleness and devastation of the things of the Spirit? Answer this to yourselves, and expel from among you those who pretend to despise the labours of Art and Science, which alone are the labours of the Gospel. Is not this plain and manifest to the thought? Can you think at all and not pronounce heartily That to Labour in Knowledge is to Build up Jerusalem, and to Despise Knowledge is to Despise Jerusalem and her Builders."[1]

In his notes to Watson's Apology, Blake asserts that

"Prophets, in the modern sense of the word, have never existed. Jonah was no prophet in the modern

[1]Pp. 703-704.

[35]

sense, for his prophecy of Nineveh failed. Every honest man is a Prophet; he utters his opinion both of private and public matters."[1]

and he sums up his opinion of the controversy between Paine and Watson as follows:

"It appears to me Now that Tom Paine is a better Christian than the Bishop.
I have read this Book with attention and find that the Bishop has only hurt Paine's heel while Paine has broken his head. The Bishop has not answer'd one of Paine's grand objections."[2]

Having thus safeguarded himself on the side of reason and reasonableness, Blake feels, no doubt, that he can indulge in the wildest flights of imagination: nothing that he will ever produce in the way of fancifulness will be beyond the reach of such interpretations. And as we find similar statements scattered all through his works, we can hope, by close work and patience, to find a key to his seemingly maddest affirmations. Blake always had a *reasonable* meaning. Only it frequently happened that he wilfully kept it hidden.
His attack on the intellect must be judged in a similar way. Blake is not against reason as such:

[1] P. 961.　　　　[2] P. 967.

[36]

Urizen and Los

(B.M. colour prints by Blake, plate 11)

he is against a perverted use of reason, which reason itself condemns.

Urizen is this abstract intellect, cut off from common sense and from imagination. In the state of innocence, Urizen and Los, Intellect and Imagination, were not—are not—separate. The first fatal division of all is the division between the two.

> "And Los, round the dark globe of Urizen,
> Kept watch for Eternals to confine
> The obscure separation alone;
> For Eternity stood wide apart,
> As the stars are apart from the earth.
>
> Los wept, howling around the dark Demon,
> And cursing his lot; for in anguish
> Urizen was rent from his side,
> And a fathomless void for his feet,
> And intense fires for his dwelling.
>
> But Urizen laid in a stony sleep,
> Unorganiz'd, rent from Eternity.
>
> The Eternals said: 'What is this? Death.
> Urizen is a clod of clay.' "[1]

Then Urizen invents abstract science.

> "He formed a line and a plummet
> To divide the Abyss beneath;
> He form'd a dividing rule;

[1] P. 247.

He formed scales to weigh,
He formed massy weights;
He formed a brazen quadrant;
He formed golden compasses,
And began to explore the Abyss."[1]

In *Jerusalem* he is defined as

"Abstract philosophy warring in enmity against Imagination."[2]

This culminates in his being called *Satan*:

". . . he is the great Selfhood, Satan."[3]

because it is he who gives separate individualities to beings. Reason makes us see things separate one from another—which is the great delusion. Thus it analyses and kills.

"Then spoke Jerusalem: 'O Albion! my Father Albion!
Why wilt thou number every little fibre of my Soul,
Spreading them out before the Sun like stalks of flax to dry?
The Infant Joy is beautiful, but its anatomy
Horrible, ghast and deadly! nought shalt thou find in it
But dark despair and everlasting brooding melancholy!' "[4]

[1]P. 255. [2]Pp. 555, cf. 562, 566, 574, 579, 552-553, 559.
[3]P. 612. [4]P. 590.

Albion under the influence of Urizen says:

" 'All these ornaments are crimes, they are made by
   the labours
Of loves, of unnatural consanguinities and friend-
   ships
Horrid to think of when enquired deeply into; and
   all
These hills and valleys are accursed witnesses of Sin
I therefore condense them into solid rocks, stedfast,
A foundation and certainty and demonstrative
   truth,
That Man be separate from Man, and here I plant
   my seat.' "[1]

Man should not be separated from Man—nor
from Woman neither, as Hamlet would have it.
We meet again with perhaps the central doctrine of Blake, the doctrine of the Unity of all
Beings: all individualisation is wrong. The
full development of the idea can only be studied
when we deal with his cosmogony. Let us mark
here only the general statement.

"Mutual in one another's love and wrath all
   renewing
We live as One Man; for contracting our infinite
   senses
We behold multitude, or expanding, we behold as
   one,

[1]Pp. 600-601.

[39]

As One Man all the Universal Family, and that One
   Man
We call Jesus the Christ; and he in us, and we in him
Live in perfect harmony in Eden, the land of life,
Giving, receiving, and forgiving each other's
   trespasses."[1]

Urizen is this contracting power of the Intellect. In cabalistic terms, he is the *retraction of God.* The Imagination is the contrary power—Los— and makes us see things as one. It must be united to Urizen: that is to say, we must see the separateness of things in this world and act accordingly, yet remember that this is only an illusion created by our mode of perception and also act accordingly.

Describing some of his visionary pictures, Blake writes:

"Here they are no longer talking of what is Good and Evil, or of what is Right or Wrong, and puzzling themselves in Satan's Labyrinth, But are Conversing with Eternal Realities as they Exist in the Human Imagination. We are in a World of Generation and death, and this world we must cast off if we would be Painters such as Rafael, Mich. Angelo and the Ancient Sculptors; if we do not cast off this world we shall be only Venetian Painters, who will be cast off and Lost from Art."[2]

[1] P. 620.   [2] Pp. 839-840, cf. 828, 830.

Abstract Intellect, left alone, kills this divine imagination:

"Imputing Sin and Righteousness to Individuals, Rahab
Sat, deep within him hid, his Feminine Power unreveal'd,
Brooding Abstract Philosophy to destroy Imagination, the Divine-Humanity:"

. . . .

"The Spectre is the Reasoning Power in Man, and when separated
From Imagination and closing itself as in steel in a Ratio
Of the Things of Memory, It thence frames Laws and Moralities
To destroy Imagination, the Divine Body, by Martyrdoms and Wars."[1]

Yet there is eternal necessity for Urizen. Let us remember the mysterious reason of his existence already given, and which can be explained only in the cosmogony:
The One would have murdered the man if he had not descended. Urizen is the necessary tool with which mankind has to do its indispensable work, and Blake when condemning intellect does not wish it suppressed, but en-

[1]Pp. 690, 699.

[41]

lightened. Thus he condemns the Deists, who conceive of God only through their cold reason and therefore wrongly.

"You, O Deists, profess yourselves the Enemies of Christianity, and you are so: you are also the Enemies of the Human Race and of Universal Nature. Man is born a Spectre or Satan and is altogether an Evil, and requires a New Selfhood continually, and must continually be changed into his direct Contrary. But your Greek Philosophy (which is a remnant of Druidism) teaches that Man is Righteous in his Vegetated Spectre: an Opinion of fatal and accursed consequence to Man, as the Ancients saw plainly by Revelation, to the intire abrogation of Experimental Theory; and many believed what they saw and Prophecied of Jesus."[1]

Thus it is that Voltaire, a deist, blasphemes:

"Voltaire insinuates that these Limits are the cruel work of God,
Mocking the Remover of Limits and the Resurrection of the Dead."[2]

But that spirit was necessary. Urizen has built the material world, and matter has been the barrier which prevented the soul from falling into nonentity in its downward flight away from God.

[1]P. 647.   [2]P. 698.

"Thus was the Mundane Shell builded by Urizen's
    strong power

.   .   .   .

For the Divine Lamb, even Jesus who is the Divine
    Vision
Permitted all, lest Man should fall into Eternal Death

.   .   .   .

Thus were the stars of heaven created like a golden
    chain,
To bind the body of Man to Heaven from falling
    into the abyss
Each took his station and his course began with
    sorrow and care."[1]

Thus Urizen is a necessary evil: he was called
upon by Albion, the Eternal Man, to do his
work; he was shaped by Imagination, Los, in
the *First Book* he is called upon by Enitharmon,
the feminine imagination. We shall see that
the whole drama of the world's history turns
round him.[2]
In Eternity, he was Faith. Luvah, Passion,
thus laments himself over Urizen's fall:

"Urizen, who was Faith and certainty, is chang'd
    to Doubt;
The hand of Urizen is upon me because I blotted out

[1]Pp. 312-313.
[2]Pp. 302, Albion; 290, 311, 312, 314, Enitharmon; 248 sq., 337,
349, Los.

That Human delusion to deliver all the sons of
    God
From bondage of the Human form. O first born Son
    of Light,
O Urizen my enemy, I weep for thy stern ambition,
But weep in vain."[1]

This necessity of doubt was also insisted upon
by Victor Hugo, and Hugo also saw in the
aberrations of the Intellect the source of all
evil.[2]
Meanwhile, in this world, Urizen is God, and
conquers all, even as the Gnostics held: Los
confessed it.

"Los answer'd in his furious pride, sparks issuing
    from his hair:
'Hitherto shalt thou come, no further; here thy
    proud waves cease.
We have drunk up the Eternal Man by our
    unbounded power,
Beware lest we also drink up thee, rough Demon of
    the waters,
Our God is Urizen the King, King of the Heavenly
    hosts;

[1] P. 306.
[2] Cf. D. Saurat: *La Religion de Victor Hugo* (Hachette):
        "Le mal avait filtré dans les hommes. Par où?
        Par l'idole."
Hugo and Blake live on the same occultist current of thought. There
are frequent similarities between them.

[44]

We have no other God but he, thou father of worms
    and clay,
And he is fall'n into the Deep, rough Demon of the
    waters,
And Los remains God over all, weak father of worms
    and clay.
I know I was Urthona, keeper of the gates of heaven,
But now I am all powerful Los, and Urthona is my
    shadow.'

Doubting stood Tharmas in the solemn darkness;
    his dim Eyes
Swam in red tears; he rear'd his waves above the
    head of Los
In wrath, but pitying back withdrew with many a
    sigh.
Now he resolv'd to destroy Los, and now his tears
    flow'd down.

In scorn stood Los, red sparks of blighting from his
    furious head
Flew over the waves of Tharmas; pitying, Tharmas
    stayed his Waves,
For Enitharmon shriek'd amain, crying: 'O my
    sweet world
Built by the Architect divine, whose love to Los and
    Enitharmon
Thou rash abhorred Demon in thy fury hast o'er-
    thrown!
'What Sovereign Architect,' said Tharmas, 'dare my
    will controll?

For if I will, I urge these waters. If I will, they sleep
In peace beneath my awful frown; my will shall be
    my Law.' "[1]

Even in his fallen state he has his function: he
preserves man from the madness of passion,
which would destroy man. In the Second Book
of *Jerusalem*, Urizen is against Luvah, Passion,
the champion of Albion, Man.[2]

Therefore he will be regenerated by the
Eternals[3] and he is already regenerated in the
elect here. This regenerated Intellect Blake
thus refers to quite clearly:

"Terrified Los sat to behold, trembling and weeping
    and howling:
'I care not whether a Man is Good or Evil; all that I
    care
Is whether he is a Wise Man or a Fool. Go, put off
    Holiness
And put on Intellect, or my thund'rous Hammer
    shall drive thee
To wrath which thou condemnest, till thou obey my
    voice.' "

.   .   .   .

"Men are admitted into Heaven not because they
have curbed and govern'd their Passions or have

[1]Pp. 330, cf. 364, 369, 371.   [2]P. 611 sq.
[3]P. 655 sq.

[46]

No Passions, but because they have Cultivated their Understandings."[1]

We have thus seen that Blake is a man of his time in his attack against the moral law and in his attack against abstract reasoning—in his curious mixture of rationalism and anti-rationalism. But in his mythological transposition of these ideas, he is following the visions of the early Gnostics, and his Urizen is closely shaped to resemble the Evil Demiurge of the first centuries of Christianity. We shall find this process of thought all through our exposition of Blake's ideas.

Blake's work is like a river into which two differently coloured streams would flow and mingle: sometimes perfectly blended, sometimes in currents separate to the eye by their colour; one is the most modern and rational thought, the other is the most ancient and fanciful mythology, or rather again a mixture of all mythologies. But if we can keep to the rational and modern stream we shall understand at least the drift and general current of the whole river: as the two streams flow together.

[1]Pp. 738-739, 842.

PART II
NATIONALISM

CELTS & DRUIDS

ADAM was a Druid, and Noah also.[1] There is perhaps no single sentence in the whole of Blake's writings which has done more harm to his reputation of sanity, and yet it is easy to give to this statement a rational meaning and thus to elucidate one of the enigmas that loom largest in his work.

Monsieur Camille Jullian (*Histoire de la Gaule,* ii. 67) gives a list of texts that bear witness to the idealisation of the Druids from antiquity to the present day. And an uninterrupted series of writers since the Alexandrians have tried to persuade the world that the source of all wisdom and virtue was in druidism. The theory was attractive for occidental pride and the Renaissance has, therefore, given a new strength to this idealisation. Milton gave a good expression of it:

"Writers of good antiquity and able judgment have been persuaded that even the school of Pythagoras

---

[1]*Descriptive Catalogue,* p. 796.

and the Persian wisdom took beginning from the old philosophy of this island."[1]

The eighteenth century, with its theories on Atlantis on the one side and its first attempts towards a systematic study of Celtic antiquity on the other, has given birth to a rich literature on this subject of the Druids. And it is easy to see by going through even a small part of that literature that Blake's ideas were not very extraordinary at the time when he wrote.

The Frenchman Pezron gave expression to the theory at the beginning of the century. He published in 1703 his book on *L'Antiquité de la Nation et de la Langue des Celts,* which was translated into English in 1706 by a Mr. Jones.

"We find, and that, upon the authority of Aristotle and Sotion, that the very rudiments of philosophy came from the Barbarians amongst whom the Celtae, or Gauls, were reckoned. And tho' Diogenes Laertius be of a contrary opinion, it is no hard matter to overthrow all his arguments, and this author makes himself ridiculous to a great degree in pretending that philosophy had its origin from the Grecians."

According to Pezron, Gomer, the eldest son of Japheth, gave birth to the Titans, who were

[1] *Areopagitica* (Bohn ed.), ii. 90.

The Serpent temples through the Earth: Los, Enitharmon, and Spectre

(*Jerusalem*, p. 100)

the ancestors of the Gauls. Their kings, Saturn, Jupiter, etc., became thereafter the gods of the Greeks, and these Titans-Gauls civilised Greece. Stukeley was celebrated about the middle of the century for his studies on Stonehenge et Abury. He identified Druidism as the religion of the patriarchs. He held that when Abraham came to Egypt he met Hercules there and made a disciple of him. Hercules was the last of the shepherd, or Hyksos, kings and he came to Western Europe and colonised Great Britain, settling there a great number of his own people, who became Druids. Blake's mention of

"The serpent Temples thro' the Earth, from the wide plain of Salisbury."[1]

shows that he knew Stukeley, who was the first to connect Stonehenge with serpent worship. But we note now a change: so far, our authors have found in the Bible the origin of their favourite races. Henceforward, with increasing frequency, the theory will be reversed and we shall find the peoples of the Bible made to descend from other nations. Respect for the Bible is giving way before erudition and national feeling.

[1]P. 712.

A little later in the century, Bailly gave to the public his celebrated theories on Atlantis. With remarkable knowledge and acumen he investigated in great detail the astronomical tables brought back from India by the missionaries and came to some conclusions which were widely advertised by his controversy with Voltaire and the *Lettres sur l'Atlantide* (1777) and *Lettres sur l'Origine des Sciences* (1777). To Bailly the Indian reckonings imply certain recurrent mistakes which prove that their observations were taken not under Indian latitudes, but at a latitude of about 49° N. Bailly inferred from that fact that the Indians did not work out these calculations themselves, but had received them through a long line of tradition from people more advanced than themselves in the sciences and whose habitate was the South of Siberia. Studying classical texts by the light of this theory, Bailly built up a complete history of pre-classical antiquity. Atlantis had been somewhere near the North Pole: Greenland, Iceland, Spitzbergen, Nova Zembla, are remnants of the Atlantic Continent. The cooling of the earth and various cosmic catastrophes drove south the Hyperboreans, a people who settled in the South of

[54]

Siberia at a latitude of about 49° and founded there a civilisation from which all other civilisations were derived. But later on, from this same northern Atlantis came out a second swarm of emigrants, the Atlants, who invaded the country of the Hyperboreans. These were scattered by the invasion and carried their civilisation to India, China, Greece, etc.

But this theory could not be accepted by our Celtomaniacs, since it explains everything without bringing in either Gauls or Druids. Therefore Bailly was violently attacked in 1777 by l'Abbé Baudeau, who published his *Mémoire à consulter pour les anciens Druides gaulois contre M. Bailly, de l'Académie des Sciences*. Baudeau explains that the real Atlants had been the Gauls and tries to twist to the advantage of his theory the ingenious detailed work done by the astronomer. In Baudeau's book we find over again Pythagoras as a pupil of the Druids, the invention of fire in the Pyrenees (demonstrated by the word-root, *Pyr*) and the source of all arts and sciences in the British Isles.

Bailly's work enjoyed a huge success in England and the whole controversy was followed with the greatest interest throughout Europe,

BLAKE AND MODERN THOUGHT

Voltaire himself taking a leading part in it. A further step was taken by the Celtomaniacs when the Welsh bard, Edward Williams, published his *Poems* in 1794. He included in the volume the celebrated Triades[1] known since 1601 (Davies: *Celtic Researches*, p. 153) and a veritable Credo:

"The Patriarchal Religion of Ancient Britain, called Druidism, . . . is no more inimical to Christianity than the religion of Noah, Job, or Abraham; it has never, as some imagine, been quite extinct in Britain; the Welsh Bards have through all ages, *down to the present*, kept it alive. . . .

Ancient British Christianity was strongly tinctured with Druidism. The Welsh Bards kept up a perpetual war with the Church of Rome. . . . Narrow understandings may conceive that they were . . . less Christian for having been Druids. The doctrine of metempsychosis is that which of all others most clearly vindicates the ways of God to Man."

Williams built on this basis a complete system of religious metaphysics, in twenty-nine articles, in which he describes a progression of the soul from reincarnation to reincarnation without showing any originality of thought.

[1]Blake mentions and quotes the *Welsh Triades* as the source of his tale of the *Three Ancient Britons* (p. 775).

Edward Davies, with his *Celtic Researches* published in 1804, is a precious witness of the ideas
that were being discussed by Blake's contemporaries. He reverts to the old theory that
the Celts were the descendants of Noah through
Gomer, the Titans and the Giants. The Druids
preserved in its purity the primitive tradition
which through Noah and Adam goes back to
God himself. (*Celtic Researches*, pp. 124, 133,
150.)

The philosophy of Greece came from the Celts,
and Pythagoras was a pupil of the Druids who
taught him the doctrine of metempsychosis;
Atlas was the son of Japheth. Hercules is not
accepted as a creditable ancestor; he was only
a barbarian whose raids wrought havoc in
the West. (Pp. 184, 193.)

But Davies goes further. He suggests that the
Druids, when they had duly taught Pythagoras,
sent him to India. And he quotes Wilford, who
had said in 1791 in a periodical (*Asiat. Rec.*
v. 3): that the Hindoos "knew of Britain by
name (Bretashtan) *as the abode of the Pitris who
were the fathers of the human race.*" These Pitris
were still alive in Great Britain and there were
still Hindoos to go to see them. In 1791, a
Hindoo, coming on a pilgrimage, had been

[57]

known to reach Moscow (pp. 193, 199), and Davies concludes triumphantly that wisdom had been given to both India and Greece by the British Isles.

However precious he may be to us when he speaks in his own name, he is more precious when he reports what others think. Some others go much further than he does. Thus, commentating upon Welsh ballads, Davies says:

"Patriarchs are made almost exclusively the fathers of the Cymry, and the general events of early ages are consigned particularly to the Island of Britain."

At the deluge:

"All mankind were drowned, except only two persons who escaped in a boat; of them was re-peopled the Island of Britain." (Pp. 153, 157, 163.)

Davies' Christian conscience is shocked at such beliefs and says that they "illustrate the nostratism of all national traditions."

But we have thus gathered together all the ideas relating to the Druids that we shall find in Blake; if we call him mad, he will be mad in good company. Noah was a Druid, since it was

[58]

in Great Britain and not on Mount Ararat that he had established his family on coming out of the Ark. As for Adam, he was obviously one of the *"Pitris" who were the fathers of the human race* and who also lived in Great Britain. Adam was thus also a Druid and the Hindoo who had come as far as Moscow was there to bear witness. Blake was not responsible for these ideas nor for the survival in the midst of the Welsh mountains of the primitive sages, since Edward Williams knew that those sages were there (he was probably one of them himself) and since Hindoos came to see them in 1791 and in 1794, long before Blake wrote his *Descriptive Catalogue*.

How did Blake know of all this? The more we study Blake, and the more persuaded we become that there was not one absurdity in Europe at the end of the eighteenth century that Blake did not know. It is infinitely probable that he frequented Swedenborgian and Occultist cenacles where whatever happened in the intellectual Europe of the time was discussed with appropriate commentaries and additions. Blake's statements have rarely a character of bookish documents. They seem rather to belong to a stock of oral communications of verbal traditions, conversations in which individual fancy enlarges upon collective divagations.

In any case we have his own statement that he knew Jacob Bryant:

"The antiquities of every Nation under Heaven, is no less sacred than that of the Jews. They are the same thing, as Jacob Bryant and all antiquaries have proved. How other antiquities came to be neglected and disbelieved, while those of the Jews are collected and arranged, is an enquiry worthy both of the Antiquarian and the Divine. All had originally one language, and one religion."[1]

This is not very helpful as really Bryant is a far more orthodox thinker than Blake, and Blake, quoting him, is obviously trying to impress his reader with his own scientific orthodoxy. But Bryant devotes a whole chapter to Pezron and is useful as a transmitter of knowledge. Also he tells much about Indians and Eastern philosophers, and quotes the *Ambassades mémorables* as follows, on Japanese ideas:

"Le monde avant la création était enfermé dans un œuf dont la coque était de métal. Cet œuf flotta longtemps sur l'eau, et fut enfin par succession de temps enveloppé d'une croûte épaisse."

[1]P. 797. Jacob Bryant, *A new system or an analysis of ancient mythology.* 1774. 3 vols.

Bryant goes on:

"We have the mundane egg upon the waters."[1]

We shall have, in our Part III, to deal again with this *mundane egg*, a rather frequent recurrence in Blake, but for other reasons.

Perhaps some of Blake's extraordinary names have partly been inspired by some of Bryant's disquisitions—we shall see later that India may also have had a part to play in the matter.

Ur (Aur, Our) is given as a root for light and fire, and Blake's *Uri*zen is the prince of Light. On, eon, refer to the Sun.

Is, az, ees, also refer to light, fire and the Sun. Zan refers to the Sun.[2]

Is it too much to imagine Blake mixing up all these sounds, Ur, is (ees), zan (eon) and coming to Urizen?

Bryant tells us also of an *Urchan*, God of fire, or *Orchan*, *Orchanes*, who might have produced Blake's *Orc*, the Terrible Child ever in flames, red Orc whose livid conflagration generally fails to bring any light into the prophecies.[3]

In Edward Jones (*Musical and poetical relicks of the Welsh Bards*, 1794) we come upon the

[1]Vol. iii. pp. 127 sq. on Pezron, p. 579 on the mundane egg.
[2]Vol. i. pp. 13, 16, 26, 35.   [3]Bryant, vol. i. p. 42.

[61]

Welsh hero Urien,[1] who may also have had an echo in Urizen. This Edward Jones was fond of proverbs somewhat Blakean in sound, and which recall some Proverbs of Hell.

> "The Eagle's strength is in his beak.
> What God made he never mars.
> No valour is equal to man's."[2]

These Welsh proverbs show us in any case a parallel in form to Blake's *Proverbs of Hell* and *Auguries of Innocence*. The second part of Jones's *Musical relicks* (1800) has for a frontispiece Gray's *Bard: On a rock whose haughty brow*. Here again, of course, Blake was one of a crowd. (P. 794 of Keynes' edition.)
The Bardic Museum quotes in the Introduction (p. vi) Milton's passage in the *Areopagitica* given above—even as Blake writes "believing with Milton the ancient British History.[3] . . ." Jones also quoted from *Paradise Regained* a line which he boldly applies to Wales (Milton had meant it for the Hebrews).

"That rather Greece from us these arts derived. . . ."

and speaks of Wales' "venerable remains . . . perhaps unparalleled in any other country."

[1]Pp. 18-19.   [2]*Bardic Museum*, 802.   [3]P. 797.

But let us now see what Blake made out of such promising elements.

Naturally, Blake adopts the extreme form of the theory. Mankind was born in the West. Adam was a Druid. Consequently Blake calls him Albion. The Druids were therefore the first of men, the founders of civilisation and of religion. The Druids are then found to be the origin of all civilisations, and especially of the most important: Jewish civilisation. The Patriarchs were Druids. We find here in process of construction the occultist legend, which was to become celebrated a little later through Fabre d'Olivet, under the name of the "Cycle of Ram"—the epic of a great Celtic migration that had started from the Atlantic and gone as far as the Pacific through the whole of the Continent, colonising and civilising on its way Greece, Palestine, Babylon, Persia, India and China. Later still the reason of this migration was to be found in the destruction of Atlantis, a catastrophe that had been foreseen by the wise, who had taken part of their people towards the East to avoid it. These conceptions were already brewing round Blake.

Thus Jerusalem was an emanation of Albion. *Jerusalem the emanation of the giant Albion.* Not only in a metaphorical or mythical sense as a feminine part of Albion's soul, but also in the historical sense, the Jews being a race that had come from Great Britain. Let us remember that about 1790 Richard Brothers had his revelations and taught the English that they were the ten lost tribes of Israel. A whole literature developed to show the identity between the Jewish race and the English race. Blake gives this idea the opposite direction, following the Celtomaniacs and making the Jews come from England.

Here is felt the influence of another myth, which we shall study in our third Part, the myth of the division and of the reconstitution of the divine hermaphrodite, a by-product of the great Plotinian tradition.

At the fall, Jerusalem was separated from Albion. At the consummation of things, Jerusalem is to be reunited to Albion, in a metaphysical sense and also in a historical sense. The Jews are to come back to England and Blake, with all the foresight of a Quartermaster-General, has allotted out the counties of Great Britain to the various tribes of Israel. The theory being thus clear, we can now study the texts.

Descriptive Catalogue: The Ancient Britons: The Britons
(say historians) were naked civilised men, learned,
studious, abstruse in thought and contemplation,
naked simple, plain in their acts and manners, wiser
than after ages. . . .

. . . The British antiquities are now in the artist's
hands. . . .

. . . Mr. B. has on his hand poems of the highest
antiquity. . . .

. . . Adam was a Druid, and Noah also; Abraham
was called to succeed the Druidical age. . . .

. . . In the meantime (Mr. B.) has painted this
picture which supposes that . . . in the fifth century
there were remains of those naked heroes in the
Welsh mountains; they are there now; Gray saw
them in the person of his bard on Snowdon; there
they dwell in naked simplicity. . . .

. . . The giant Albion was Patriarch of the Atlantic;
he is the Atlas of the Greeks, one of those the Greeks
call Titans. . . .

Vision of the Last Judgment: "He is Albion, our Ancestor, patriarch of the Atlantic Continent, whose
history preceded that of the Hebrews." (P. 834.)

Blake is speaking of Atlantis. *The Atlantic
Continent,* whose history came before that of
the Hebrews; Adam, the first man the Hebrews
knew of, was a Druid come from Atlantis. The
science of the time, with Bailly, was looking for
the origin of races and civilisations outside the

Bible, whereas fifty or a hundred years earlier, Pezron or Stukeley were still attempting to make the Celts come from Gomer or Abraham. Noah also was a Druid. In the Welsh Triades, which so scandalised Davies, Noah settled in Great Britain. Consequently, he was not a survivor of the Biblical deluge, but of the ruin of Atlantis, since Great Britain is a fragment of the fabulous Continent. The legend is in full process of construction at the end of the eighteenth century—if we are to go by the texts. Orally, it is probably fully formed already among the initiated occultists and Celtomaniacs, since the written tradition frequently comes a good bit later than the early teaching in occultism. In Blake we find only allusions and fragments, because allusions were sufficient to those for whom he wrote. Blake's aim is not to tell us of the tradition, but to tell those who know of it already what his own individual revelations have added to it. Hence, Blake's obscurity to the non-initiated. For a Swedenborgian, for an occultist of the clubs frequented by Blake, his allusions would have been very clear. But the occultist tradition, which is not generally written down, varies with a rapidity, greater, perhaps, than any other tradition.

Consequently, we are only making an attempt at guessing what these people might be thinking at the end of the eighteenth century, and we are helped only by insufficient texts. And yet, here lies the only explanation of Blake's ideas.

Let us note another trait. The heroes of this tradition were still living in the Welsh mountains. Williams had said, "Down to the present" in 1794; Blake said, "they are there now." Nothing in this clear statement of the Catalogue belongs personally to Blake.

It is useless to gather all the allusions to the Druids which can be found in Blake's works. They teach us nothing more.[1]

But the poem entitled *Jerusalem* is to be examined in the light of these ideas, because the subject of Jerusalem is precisely this subject: how did Jerusalem come from Albion, how did the Jews come from Great Britain and how are they to come back to it?

Can we find in *Jerusalem* and the *Prophetic Books* generally any allusions to the catastrophe of Atlantis? From the point of view of the texts, the legend is only in a state of construction.

[1]Here is a list of references: Albion Snowdon 298, Druids 221, 237, 238, 304-5, 597-598; —466 bards, 471, 477, 478, 481, 528, 658, 662, 670-679, 680, 689, 740; —553, 564, 588, 595, 652; —611, 621, 630; —564, 596, 626, 638 sq., 650, 771, 794, 796 (naked heroes), 794, 834.

But it is a catastrophe that annihilates Great Britain and scatters its priests as far as Palestine and Egypt. We recognise at the beginning of *Jerusalem* the fragments of the classical tale:

"In all the dark Atlantic vale down from the hills of
Surrey
A black water accumulates. . . .
Albion's mountains run with blood, the cries of war
and tumult
Resound into the unbounded night. . . .
Jerusalem is scatter'd like a cloud of smoke. . . .
Moab and Ammon and Amalek and Canaan and
Egypt and Aram
Receive her little ones for sacrifices and the delights
of cruelty."[1]

Blake merely adds to the traditional story his condemnation of formal religion, identified again with that of the Old Testament, since he frequently considers Jehovah as his personal enemy. At the end of the poem, the description of Albion in his state of abasement is also reminiscent of the engulfed Atlantis:

"Albion cold lays on his Rock; storms and snows
beat round him
Howling winds cover him: roaring seas dash furious
against him;

[1] *Jerusalem*, pp. 552-553.

[68]

In the deep darkness broad lightnings, long thunders
    roll.
The weeds of Death inwrap his hands and feet,
    blown incessant
And washed incessant by the forever restless sea-
    waves, foaming abroad
Upon the white rock. . . .
And the body of Albion was closed apart from all
    Nations."[1]

Since "The Giant Albion was patriarch of the
Atlantic, he is the Atlas of the Greeks."[2]
Blake is obviously describing an oceanic catastrophe and the associations between Albion
asleep on the Rock of Ages and Atlantis over-
whelmed by the sea are unavoidable.

"And the voices of Bath and Canterbury and York
    and Edinburgh, cry
Over the Plow of Nations in the strong hand of
    Albion, thundering along
Among the Fires of the Druid and the deep black
    rethundering Waters
Of the Atlantic which poured in impetuous loud,
    loud, louder and louder,
And the great voice of the Atlantic howled over the
    Druid Altars."[3]

[1] *Jerusalem*, p. 742.   [2] P. 797.
[3] *Jerusalem*, p. 657.

Here is now an allusion to what had gone before the catastrophe:

"Therefore remove from Albion these terrible
Surfaces
And let wild seas and rocks close up Jerusalem away
from
The Atlantic Mountains where giants dwelt in
Intellect,
Now given to stony Druids. . . ."[1]

In *America*, we find another clear allusion:

"On those vast shady hills between America and
Albion's shore
Now barr'd out by the Atlantic sea, call'd Atlantean
hills,
Because from their bright summits you may pass to
the Golden world,
An ancient palace, archetype of mighty Emperies,
Rears its immortal pinnacles, built in the forest of God
By Ariston, the king of beauty, for his stolen bride.

Here on their magic seats the thirteen Angels sat
perturb'd
For clouds from the Atlantic hover o'er the solemn
roof."[2]

We are here

"Above Time's troubled Fountains
On the great Atlantic mountains

[1] *Jerusalem*, p. 645.   [2] P. 222.

[70]

In my golden House on high
There they shine eternally."[1]

Los seems to have been concerned in this whelming of the Atlantis:

"Los in his wrath curs'd heaven and earth; he rent
  up Nations,
Standing on Albion's rocks among high-rear'd
  Druid temples
Which reach the stars of heaven and stretch from
  pole to pole.
He displac'd continents, the oceans fled before his
  face:
He alter'd the poles of the world, east, west and
  north and south,
But he clos'd up Enitharmon from the sight of these
  things."[2]

and again:

"The Atlantic Continent sunk round Albion's
  cliffy shore,
And the Sea poured in amain upon the Giants of
  Albion
As Los bended the Senses of Reuben."[3]

We must note here that for Blake, not only was Noah a Druid, but he was the last of the real Druids: those who remained in the West after the catastrophe became the representatives of

[1]P. 127.   [2]P. 478.   [3]P. 618.

a cruel and degenerate religion—"stony Druids" as Blake calls them. This downfall rendered the coming of Abraham necessary, as we have seen:

"Abraham was called to succeed the Druidical age, which began to turn allegorical and mental signification into corporal command, whereby human sacrifice would have depopulated the earth."[1]

We are, however, forced to admit that some of these Druids had not yet degenerated, since they were still to be found as *naked heroes* in Blake's time. We must also admit that Blake could contradict himself occasionally.

But whether he praises them or blames them, the Druids started from England to civilise the world.

"And London walked in every Nation, mutual in Love and harmony—Albion cover'd the whole Earth, England encompassed the nations."[2]

"Return, return to Lambeth's Vale, O building of human souls!
Thence stony Druid Temples overspread the Island white,
And thence from Jerusalem's ruins, from her walls of salvation

[1] *Descriptive Catalogue.*   [2] *Jerusalem*, p. 595.

[72]

And praise, tho' the whole Earth were rear'd from
Ireland
To Mexico and Peru west, and east to China and
Japan, till Babel
The Spectre of Albion frown'd over the Nations in
glory and war.
All things begin and end in Albions ancient Druid
rocky shore."[1]

And Blake tells the deists: "Your Greek
philosophy . . . is a remnant of Druidism."[2]
Having thus stated the general idea, we can go
on to Blake's application of it to the Jews.
Blake tells them in prose between Chapters I.
and II. of *Jerusalem*:

"Jerusalem the Emanation of the Giant Albion!
Can it be? Is it a Truth that the Learned[3] have
explored? Was Britain the Primitive Seat of the
Patriarchal Religion? If it is true, my title-page is
also True, that Jerusalem was and is the Emanation
of the Giant Albion. It is True, and cannot be con-

---

[1]P. 472. *Lambeth*, because in this poem, *Milton*, Blake is largely
personal and explains chiefly how *he*, *Blake*, came to have to do, or
complement, Milton's work of prophecy, and to be partly a reincarnation of Milton, or at least a new form of the same spirit that was in
Milton. And Blake lived in Lambeth.

[2]P. 647.

[3]*The learned* are the various authors we have quoted and from whom
he gathered all that follows. Abraham, the altars of stone, the
"druidical" stones and the oaks are frequently connected ideas in
all this literature.

troverted. Ye are united, O ye Inhabitants of Earth, in One Religion: The Religion of Jesus: the most Ancient, the Eternal and the Everlasting Gospel. The Wicked will turn it to Wickedness, the Righteous to Righteousness. Amen! Huzza! Selah!

Your Ancestors derived their origin from Abraham, Heber, Shem, and Noah, who were Druids: as the Druid Temples (which are the Patriarchal Pillars and Oak Groves) over the whole Earth witness to this day.

You have a tradition, that Man anciently contain'd in his mighty limbs all things in Heaven and Earth: this you received from the Druids.

But now the Starry Heavens are fled from the mighty limbs of Albion.

Albion was the Parent of the Druids: and in his Chaotic State of Sleep Satan and Adam and the whole World was Created by the Elohim."

He soars then into verse, more enthusiastic still, less clear, it is true, but on the same general theme:

> "The fields from Islington to Marylebone,
> To Primrose Hill and Saint John's Wood,
> Were builded over with pillars of gold
> And there Jerusalem's pillars stood.
>
> .   .   .   .
>
> The Jew's-harp-house and the Green Man,
> The Ponds where Boys to bathe delight,

[74]

The fields of Cows by William's farm
Shine in Jerusalem's pleasant sight.

She walks upon our meadows green:
The Lamb of God walks by her side:
And every English Child is seen,
Children of Jesus and his Bride."

And he ends in prose again on a clear allusion
to the doctrines of the Adam-Kadmon of the
Cabala, the division of the primitive Giant
from whom all beings have been drawn by
sacrifice. He follows the Christian tradition
begun by Pico della Mirandola, and tries to use
the Cabala to convert the Jews.

"If Humanity is Christianity, you, O Jews, are the
true Christians; if your tradition that Man contained in his limbs all Animals is True and they were
separated from him by cruel sacrifices; and when
compulsory cruel Sacrifices had brought Humanity
into a Feminine Tabernacle, in the loins of Abraham
and David, the Lamb of God, the Saviour became
apparent on Earth as the Prophets had foretold!
The Return of Israel is a Return to Mental Sacrifice
and War. Take up the Cross, O Israel, and follow
Jesus."

Thus the Jews have gone from England. Blake
knows all about this exodus. They ran away at
the time of the conflict between Luvah and

Urizen, that is to say, at the time of the
Fall:

"... When they fled out at Jerusalem's Gates,
Away from the conflict of Luvah and Urizen, fixing
the Gates
In the Twelve Counties of Wales and thence Gates
looking every way,
To the four Points, conduct to England and Scotland
and Ireland,
And thence to all the Kingdoms and Nations and
Families of the Earth."

And Blake gives the places they come from or
the places they went through (this is not very
clear) according to their tribes:

"The Gate of Reuben in Carmarthenshire: the Gate
of Simeon in
Cardiganshire: and the Gate of Levi in Montgomery-
shire:
The Gate of Judah, Merionethshire: the Gate of
Dan, Flintshire:
The Gate of Naphtali, Radnorshire: the Gate of
Gad, Pembrokeshire:
The Gate of Asher, Carnarvonshire: the Gate of
Issachar, Brecknokshire:
The Gate of Zebulun, in Anglesea and Sodor, so is
Wales divided,
The Gate of Joseph, Denbighshire: the Gate of
Benjamin, Glamorganshire:

[76]

For the protection of the Twelve Emanations of
Albion's Sons.
And the Forty Counties of England are thus divided
in the Gates:
Of Reuben, Norfolk, Suffolk, Essex: Simeon, Lincoln,
York, Lancashire:
Levi, Middlesex, Kent, Surrey: Judah, Somerset,
Glouster, Wiltshire.
Dan, Cornwall, Devon, Dorset."

And he goes on to the end of the tribes and of
the counties.
However, some among the sons of Jerusalem
remain in Great Britain and in Ireland:

"Because Twelve Sons of Jerusalem fled successive
thro' the Gates,
But the Four Sons of Jerusalem who fled not but
remain'd
Are Rintrah and Palamabron and Theotormon and
Bromion,
The Four that remain with Los to guard the Western
Wall:
And these Four remain to guard the Four Walls of
Jerusalem,
Whose foundations remain in the Thirty-two Counties
of Ireland,
And in the Twelve Counties of Wales, and in the
Forty Counties
Of England, and in the Thirty-six Counties of
Scotland.

And the names of the Thirty-two Counties of Ireland
  are these:
Under Judah and Issachar and Zebulum are Lowth,
  Londford,
Eastmeath, Westmeath, Dublin, Kildare, King's
  County,
Queen's County, Wicklow, Catherloh, Wexford,
  Kilkenny:
And those under Reuben and Simeon and Levi are
  these."[1]

And here Blake puts in another catalogue,
similar to the first one. Then his vision widens
and he explains that it was not only the Jews who
came from England, but that all the nations
of the Earth did so, and that all the nations of
the Earth must come back to England:

"All these Center in London and in Golgonooza,
  from whence
They are Created continually, East and West and
  North and South:
And from them are Created all the Nations of the
  Earth,
Europe and Asia and Africa and America, in fury
  Fourfold!
And Thirty-two the Nations, to dwell in Jerusalem's
  Gates.
O come ye Nations, Come ye People, Come up to
  Jerusalem.

[1]P. 695.

[78]

Return, Jerusalem, and dwell together as of old:
Return,
Return: O Albion, let Jerusalem overspread all
Nations,
As in the times of old; O Albion awake! Reuben
wanders,
The Nations wait for Jerusalem, they look up for the
Bride.
France, Spain, Italy, Germany, Poland, Russia,
Sweden, Turkey,
Arabia, Palestine, Persia, Hindostan, China, Tartary,
Siberia.[1]

The Fall into the World is thus described:

"Such is the Ancient World of Urizen in the Satanic
Void,
Created from the Valley of Middlesex by London's
River,
From Stone-henge and from London Stone, from
Cornwall to Cathnes.
The Four Zoas rush around on all sides in dire ruin:
Furious in pride of Selfhood the terrible Spectres of
Albion
Rear their dark Rocks among the Stars of God,
stupendous
Works! A World of Generation continually Creating
out of
The Hermaphroditic Satanic World of rocky
destiny."[2]

[1]P. 696.   [2]P. 660, 682 sq.

Let us listen now to the lamentations of Jerusalem on the banks of the Euphrates. England is the theme of her song.

"How distant far from Albion! his hills and his valleys no more
Receive the feet of Jerusalem: they have cast me quite away:
And Albion is himself shrunk to a narrow rock in the middle of the sea!
The plains of Sussex and Surrey, their hills of flocks and herds,
No more seek to Jerusalem nor to the sound of my Holy-ones.
The Fifty-two Counties of England are harden'd against me
As if I was not their Mother, they despise me and cast me out.
London cover'd the whole Earth, England encompass'd the Nations,
And all the Nations of the Earth were seen in the Cities of Albion.

. . . .

Albion gave me to the whole Earth to walk up and down; to pour
Joy upon every mountain, to teach songs to the shepherd and plowman.
I taught the ships of the sea to sing the songs of Zion.
Italy saw me, in sublime astonishment; France was wholly mine,

As my garden and as my secret bath; Spain was my
    heavenly couch,
I slept in his golden hills; the Lamb of God met me
    there."[1]

But at last regeneration comes to the Nations
of the Earth, and especially the Jews come back
into the new Jerusalem, which is England.
The sons of Jerusalem that had remained in
England reconstruct the divine city. Blake,
naturally, is one of the chief workmen—perhaps
the chief workman.

"Highgate's heights and Hampstead's, to Poplar,
    Hackney and Bow;
To Islington and Paddington and the Brook of
    Albion's River.
We builded Jerusalem as a City and a Temple; from
    Lambeth
We began our Foundations; lovely Lambeth, O
    lovely Hills."[2]

Los sees and announces the final triumph, the
reintegration of multiplicity into unity, the
reconstruction of the One, the return to Great
Britain:

"So Los terrified cries; trembling and weeping and
    howling: Beholding.

  .   .   .   .

[1]P. 708.   [2]P. 722.

What do I see! The Briton, Saxon, Roman, Norman
amalgamating
In my furnaces into One Nation, the English: and
taking refuge
In the Loins of Albion. The Canaanite united with
the fugitive
Hebrew, whom she divided into Twelve, and sold
into Egypt,
Then scatter'd the Egyptian and Hebrew to the
four Winds."[1]

The time has come. England awakes, and, as
in the days of the Creation, will become again
the whole world. A strange mystic imperialism,
which reveals, at the back of the fantastic
unfolding of the imagination of Blake, one of
the most fundamental characteristics of the
Anglo-Saxon race.

"Time was Finished! The Breath Divine Breathed
over Albion
Beneath the Furnaces and starry Wheels and in the
Immortal Tomb
And England who is Brittannia awoke from Death
on Albion's bosom."[2]

Albion rouses himself from his sleep through
the ages and becomes Man:

[1]P. 739.   [2]P. 743.

". . . Then Albion stood before Jesus in the Clouds
Of Heaven, Fourfold among the Visions of God in
    Eternity.

.   .   .   .

Awake, Awake, Jerusalem! O lovely Emanation of
    Albion,
Awake, and overspread all Nations as in Ancient
    Time.
For lo! the Night of Death is past and the Eternal
    Day
Appears upon our Hills: Awake, Jerusalem, and come
    away!
So spake the Vision of Albion, and in him so spake
    in my hearing
The Universal Father. Then Albion stretch'd his
    hand into Infinitude,
And took his Bow. . . ."[1]

The great epic, *Jerusalem*, runs on other themes
also, the division and the reconstitution of the
One, the wars of the Sexes, the revolt of the
soul against dogma and morality and so on.
But the conducting thread of this labyrinth is
in the legendary history of the Celtic race, as
the Celtomaniacs of the eighteenth century
imagined it. Blake's story is shapen by his
mind, so precise and so fantastic at the same
time, pouring down upon the reader a shower

[1]P. 747.

[83]

of astounding details, which yet have a curious logic about them. Once the general thesis is admitted, why not imagine facts in detail; why not divide up the counties of England among the tribes of Israel? This theory does not explain everything in *Jerusalem*, but it helps us to understand the general scheme of the poem. It helps us to understand a little better the poet's enthusiasm and, secondly, to enjoy with less misgiving his wonderful flights, as when he cries:

"And did those feet in ancient time
  Walk upon England's mountains green?
And was the holy Lamb of God
  On England's pleasant pastures seen?

And did the Countenance Divine
  Shine forth upon our clouded hills?
And was Jerusalem builded here
  Among these dark Satanic Mills?

Bring me my bow of burning gold!
  Bring me my arrows of desire!
Bring me my spear! O clouds, unfold!
  Bring me my chariots of fire!

I will not cease from mental fight,
  Nor shall my sword sleep in my hand,
Till we have built Jerusalem
  In England's green and pleasant land."[1]

[1] P. 464.

We can now understand this marvellous lyric. Jesus is the primitive and the total man reconstituted. On his second coming he was manifest in Palestine, but at the time of his first existence before the Fall, he was Albion. Primitive humanity was formed in England, and in England humanity will reach its supreme goal. The old dream of the Celtomaniacs lives in Blake and lives, perhaps, at the bottom of every English soul. It is a fragment of that faith in themselves which makes nations great.

PART III
PANTHEISTIC IDEALISM

WE come now to the hardest part of our task. So far, we have dealt with two strands in Blake's tangle that could be fairly easily separated from the rest. We are now face to face with the central chaos. What is Blake's cosmogony?

I shall first attempt to explain as much as I may from outside parallelisms, and to find in the Gnostics, in the Cabalists, in the Hindoos, as much light as can be brought to bear on Blake. This will clear several roads into the tangle. But then we shall have to penetrate into the heart of the wood, and guess at what we cannot see. But perhaps, after our several inroads, we shall find that a certain amount of light has penetrated even into the darkest places.

I. PARALLELISMS

1. THE GNOSTICS

MOSHEIM will clear a considerable part of the very obscure tale told in the first prophetic books. Let us follow his account without taking much notice of the individual gnostic sects to whom the ideas belong. Blake obviously never cared whom his ideas came from.

—From God come Aeons, who produce other Aeons. (Mosheim, ii. 227.)

—The last who lives near the abyss, conceives the idea of creating a material world; he has compeers, and becomes worshipped as a God.

—God adds to man, created by this process, an intelligent and rational soul, much impeded by that brutal soul derived from matter (233).

—The supreme God sends prophets to save men (235).

—And at last sends his son Nus to end the reign of inferior spirits (237).

Thus far Basilides according to Mosheim.

This gives us the Eternals in Blake, as the Aeons; the last of them is Urizen, who will create the material world, and is worshipped as a God.

But Los, the spirit of prophecy, hovers round Urizen and his creation, to awake men's souls. Thus the general theme of the first prophetic books is clear. But Mosheim's Valentine will take us much further into the details. The aeons were arranged in couples: male and female, and there were four couples. Thus in Blake we have the four Zoas and their four female emanations (Mosheim, ii. 273, 274).

Now Sophia, the last aeon, wishing to contemplate the Father, rushes away from the Pleroma[1] and would be lost in nonentity, but that one Horos (the limit) or Horus intervenes and stops her. (ii. 281.)

Thus to the descent of Urizen, limits have been set. Sophia has four passions, which caused her fall: ignorance, pain, terror, despair. These correspond to the moods of Blake's four Zoas: Urizen is ignorance, Luvah is suffering, Los is terror, Tharmas is despair: these connotations follow them throughout the *Prophetic Books*. Much else goes to the making

[1]A similar tale is told in the *Zohar* (de Pauly, vol. i. p. 119).

of the Zoas, but these moods are very clearly
in with the rest.

Mosheim continues (ii. 281).

"This violent commotion, however, was productive
of an effect which it was utterly out of the power of
Horus to prevent, namely, that Sophia was delivered
of a daughter styled Achamoth, who, being expelled
from the Pleroma, was immersed in the rude and
chaotic mass of unformed matter which lay without
it."

This daughter

"lay at first in a very miserable form, being utterly
destitute of either form, figure or light."

But Christ "imparted to her somewhat of
form, intelligence and rationality." (ii. 283.)
She tried to get near to the Pleroma, but
Horus, the guardian of the borders, prevented
her. So her cries, smiles, etc., create the elements, water, light, air, earth: "all the elements
of the world from her sorrows and despondency" till Christ comes again to her help.
In Blake, Urizen plays the part of both Sophia
and Achamoth, and Los the part of Christ.
The Eternals play the part of Horus.
The Eternals are horrified at the Birth, like

[93]

Horus, and powerless to prevent it; but deter-
mined to separate themselves from it:

> "All Eternity shudder'd at sight
> Of the first female now separate,
> Pale as a cloud of snow
> Waving before the face of Los.
>
> Wonder, awe, fear, astonishment
> Petrify the eternal myriads
> At the first female form now separate.
> They call'd her Pity, and fled.
>
> 'Spread a Tent with strong curtains around them.
> Let cords and stakes bind in the Void,
> That Eternals may no more behold them.'
>
> They began to weave curtains of darkness,
> They erected large pillars round the Void,
> With golden hooks fasten'd in the pillars
> With infinite labour the Eternals
> A woof wove, and called it Science."

· · · · · · · · ·

> "The Eternals their tent finished
> Alarm'd with these gloomy visions,
> When Enitharmon groaning
> Produc'd a man Child to the light.
>
> A shriek ran thro' Eternity
> And a paralytic stroke,
> At the birth of the Human shadow.

[94]

Delving earth in his resistless way,
Howling, the Child with fierce flames
Issu'd from Enitharmon.

The Eternals closed the tent;
They beat down the stakes, the cords

Stretch'd for a work of eternity,
No more Los beheld Eternity."[1]

This horror of the Birth of Man we shall find
again in Hindoo mythology as Blake knew it.
But Christ does not give up the fallen world.
Thus Los remains round the world of Urizen:
to watch and to help: to impart "somewhat of
form, intelligence and rationality":

"And Los, round the dark globe of Urizen,
Kept watch for Eternals to confine
And obscure separation alone;
For Eternity stood wide apart,
As the stars are apart from the earth."[2]

Los binds Urizen and thus shapes him:

"The Eternal Prophet heav'd the dark bellows,
And turn'd restless the tongs, and the hammer
Incessant beat, forging chains new and new,
Numb'ring with links hours, days and years."[3]

We have seen that Imagination has thus its

[1]Pp. 252-253, 254.   [2]P. 247.   [3]P. 248.

part in the shaping of the intellect. Now "these were the changes of Urizen": even as in the changes of Achamoth, whence come "all the elements of the world from her sorrows and despondency."

"The Eternal mind, bounded, began to roll
Eddies of wrath ceaseless round and round,
And the sulphureous foam, surging thick,
Settled, a lake, bright and shining clear,
White as the snow on the mountains cold.

Forgetfulness, dumbness, necessity,
In chains of the mind locked up,
Like fetters of ice shrinking together,
Disorganiz'd, rent from Eternity,

. . . .

In a horrible, dreamful slumber,
Like the linked infernal chain,
A vast Spine writh'd in torment
Upon the winds, shooting pain'd
Ribs, like a bending cavern;
And bones of solidness froze
Over all his nerves of joy.
And a first Age passed over,
And a state of dismal woe."[1]

There are seven such ages, when the world is shaped from Urizen, Los watching; and Los

[1]P. 249.

feels the same pity that the gnostic Christ
feels:

> "Los wept obscur'd with mourning,
> His bosom earthquak'd with sighs;
> He saw Urizen deadly black
> In his chains bound, and Pity began."[1]

Then something happens to Los which is
cabalistic rather than gnostic: he divides into
male and female—and at this birth also the
Eternals shudder and close their tent: Blake
complicates the myth, but on the same lines.
Yet again, Los, as Christ, pities:

> "But Los saw the Female, and pitied."[2]

Thus the pity of Los has first helped Urizen
to shape himself, and to create his world, then
helped the Female, Enitharmon, from whom
shall spring the Blakean Christ, the Saviour of
the world.

We have thus a key to practically the whole of
the *First Book of Urizen* and to much that
happens in the *Prophetic Books*. The Cabala
will explain the other element, the division into
male and female, in the *Book of Urizen*, which
will thus stand clear and be a good basis for an
understanding of the *Prophetic Books*.

[1]P. 251.   [2]P. 253.

[97]

2. THE CABALA

The Jewish Cabala is mainly known to us by the *Zohar*, an enormous compilation of texts obviously varied in origin, in antiquity and in purport, and given to the world at the beginning of the fourteenth century by a Spanish Jew, Moses of Leon. Many rumours are to be picked up in the later Middle Ages as to the secret wisdom of the Hebrews, but nothing precise can be known until Picodella Mirandola, at the end of the fifteenth century, proclaimed himself a Christian Cabalist and popularised some of the secret lore. He was eagerly followed in many lands by such minds as Reuchlin, Agrippa, Voysin, and in England Fludd made the essential ideas of the Cabala fairly widely known. Henry More, the leader of the Cambridge Platonists, was a Cabalist, and was largely instrumental in causing Knorr von Rosenroth to publish in Latin in the late seventeenth century a translation of the essential parts of the *Zohar*. It is only at the beginning of the twentieth century, however, that the first complete translation into a European language was published by de Pauly in the six volumes of the French *Zohar*.

It is impossible as yet to assess precisely the influence of this Jewish religious movement on the Western mind. That it has been great is indubitable; and this is partly due to a mis-understanding: at the Renaissance, the papacy encouraged the study of the Cabala under the misconception that it contained proofs of the truth of Christianity—proofs which the few elect among the Jews kept to themselves, but which, when made public, would bring the mass of the Jewish people into the fold of the Roman Church. We may note that this desire to convert the Jews is present in Blake, in the peculiar form of that theory of his that at the consummation of things the Jews will come back—not to Rome—but to England.

It was soon found that the Cabala held no such proofs; but the harm was done. An immense popularity among the learned had been given to this body of Jewish lore and speculation. This acted in several ways. The *Zohar* is a strange mixture of the wildest tales obviously of folk-lore origin, at times without any philoso-phical meaning whatever, of the most extra-ordinary superstitions, of the most imaginative myths, and at times of the profoundest meta-physical conceptions. So every different mind

[99]

can draw whatever it prefers from the fascinating medley.

We are, perhaps, in danger of over estimating the influence of the Cabala, owing to the fact that it is the one very large body of occultist tradition which can be directly approached. Another important source is in the Hermetic Books. But the *Hermes trismegistus* is a small collection compared to the *Zohar*: not more, perhaps, than one-twentieth of its length. Besides, all the important ideas of the Hermetic books are in the *Zohar* in a Jewish garb; and naturally the *Zohar* enlightens us on many points to which no reference is made in *Hermes*. So that the *Zohar* is our great encyclopaedia of occultism and we are tempted to use it to explain many things which perhaps come from other, though parallel, sources. For instance, there is hardly anything in the general ideas of H. P. Blavatsky which cannot be explained by the *Zohar*, if we allow for a rather slight admixture of Indian lore. So we are tempted to say that Madame Blavatsky, although rather contemptuous in her tone towards the Cabala, derived most of her ideas from it. Perhaps this is not fair to her; but until we have more documents, how can we judge? It seems to me that in any case the *Zohar* is to be used as a witness, if not as a source. We can say to any occultist: "This is already in the *Zohar* and is therefore at least as old as the thirteenth century to our certain knowledge; how you came by it, we cannot tell if you will not tell us; but, obscure and occult as you are, we can understand this much of your ideas, that the Cabala has already explained."

Thus we find that some of Milton's ideas, otherwise unexplainable, become clear; that much of Hugo's puzzling metaphysics is at least made coherent.

And thus it is with Blake.

Blake mentions the Cabala and gives us a starting point: in his address to the Jews, he says:

"You have a tradition, that Man anciently contain'd in his mighty limbs all things in Heaven and Earth: this you received from the Druids. . . .

Albion was the Parent of the Druids, and in his Chaotic State of Sleep, Satan and Adam and the whole World was Created by the Elohim."

. . . .

"If your tradition that Man contained in his Limbs all Animals is True, and they were separated from him by cruel Sacrifices, and when compulsory cruel

[101]

Sacrifices had brought Humanity into a Feminine Tabernacle in the loins of Abraham and David, the Lamb of God, the Saviour became apparent on Earth as the Prophets had foretold, The Return of Israel is a Return to Mental Sacrifice and War."[1]

We find here Adam Kadmon, the Total Man of the Cabala, whom Blake calls Albion for reasons we have seen. We find a second element, the allusion to the Feminine tabernacle, which will bring us to the sexual law of the Cabala; we shall have to follow this in detail later as we study Blake's cosmogony. We find the division of Man into all men, and animals, and *all things in heaven and Earth.* We shall see this link up with pantheistic idealism.

In short, Blake drew from the Cabala two of the greatest leading ideas of his mythology:

The Idea of the One Being from whom all beings are drawn;

The Idea of the division into Male and Female. We shall see that the Cabala explains much more of the detail of Blake's visions. Indeed the Cabalistic element is so closely woven into the very fabric of the *Prophetic Books* that it is only in studying Blake's system as a whole that we

[1]Pp. 597-600.

shall be able to judge of the influence of the
Cabala upon him.

Let us sketch here very rapidly the chief events
of his mythology:

*Before the Fall, everything was in Adam Kadmon or
Albion*: this we may explain by the Cabala.

Beings were drawn from Albion by cruel sacrifices: this
is hard to explain on Cabalistic lines; there is
one text about Cain and Abel, which we shall
study later, but which would be insufficient:
I am therefore inclined to see in these *cruel
sacrifices* a Hindoo influence, as explained below;
the Druidic legends of human sacrifice no doubt
helped also.

*Man was divided and beings were divided into Male
and Female*: this is found both in the Cabala and
in Hindooism; but then in Blake *the Female fled
from the Male*—and traces of this I cannot find
in the Cabala, where the legitimate union of
the sexes is highly praised and sought after
and regarded as sacred; where as the Hindoo
myth of Prajapati and Ushas corresponds
closely to the Blakean myth. On this second
point also, therefore, I suspect a Hindoo influence.

Then follow the wars between the four Zoas: this is
of mixed origin, classical mythology, Christian

[103]

legends of the war in Heaven, Hindoo wars among the gods all intervening.

Lastly, the Saviour is produced, and the One is reconstituted. Here again we can see the occultist theories derived probably from Plotinus's metaphysics of *the One,* its disintegration and reconstitution; also the Cabala; also the Hindoo reconstitution of Agni through the Sacrifice.

The Cabala thus explains everything (or comes in the explanation of everything) except the *cruel sacrifices* and the *refusal and flight of the Female*—two points which we shall reserve for the present.

What could Blake know of the Cabala?

The obvious answer is that he could read, in the Latin, *the Kabbala Denudata* of Knorr von Rosenroth, published in 1677-1684, and very popular among the English learned, owing to the participation of Henry More in the production and even the writing of the Book. Rosenroth gives a translation of the most important books of the *Zohar,* and reveals a sufficient amount of the Cabala to account for anything cabalistic that may be found in Blake.

One passage will be enough to cover what Blake has told us of the Cabala. We find here

the One Man, his division and even the sacri-
fice. (Rosenroth, vol. ii. p. 507, translated by
Mathers, London. Pp. 241-242.) Cain sacrifices
Abel, then

1048. "God was stirred up . . . and took him away
and placed him in the mouth of the great
abyss and enclosed his brother

1049. by immersion[1] in the great sea so that he
might temperate the supernal tears

1050. And from them men descend in the world
according to their path,

1051. And although they are concealed, yet are they
extended mutually in themselves and from
one body

1052. And from that body descend the souls of the
impious, the sinners.

1053. From them both at once? No, but one flowed
down from the one side and another from the
other.

1054. Blessed are the just, whose souls are drawn
from that Holy Body which is called Adam,
which includeth all things."

In this conception, Abel and Cain are the two
sides of Adam: the Side of Rigour and the Side
of Pity (God himself is similarly divided).
And further (Idra Rabba 1081 and 1084,

---

[1]This certainly recalls the immersion of Albion in the Atlantic
described above.

Mathers, p. 245), we are told that evil spirits
came from Cain's body:

1081. "had gone forth from the ordered arrangement of the body, which is called the inferior
Cain."
1084. "But from the spirit which is called Abel
others go forth which have been more miti-
gated."

Hence we may say that Abel in 1084 is the
Adam of 1054. Thus the *cruel sacrifices* of
Blake would mean the sacrifice of Abel by
Cain, which caused the division of the One
Adam into many beings, some good and some
evil.

But this is very complicated. Of course Blake
may have had oral commentaries, of which we
can know nothing. The theory of the *One
Original Man*, of *his division into beings*, is clear
enough throughout the Cabala. The theory of
sacrifice as the origin I have found only in this
obscure passage and feel, therefore, the need
of further support to explain the importance
given to it by Blake.

This brings us to the Hindoos.

3. THE HINDOOS

Here again we have Blake's statement that he knew India. In the *Descriptive Catalogue*, we read:

THE BRAMINS—A DRAWING

"The subject is, Mr. Wilkin translating the Geeta; an ideal design, suggested by the first publication of that part of the Hindoo Scriptures translated by Mr. Wilkin. I understand that my Costume is incorrect, but in this I plead the authority of the ancients, who often deviated from the Habits to preserve the Manners, as in the instance of the Laocoon, who, though a priest, is represented naked."[1]

Blake knew of the *Bhagavad Gita*, and he had been in contact with people who knew enough of India to tell him that his costumes were wrong. We have also seen already that the Celtic antiquarians connected India with Great Britain. Voltaire himself had fought out with Bailly the question of the origin of civilisation, and Voltaire held that all arts and philosophy came from India.[2]

Blake has told us similarly that *all religions are one*, and that the *antiquities of all nations are one*.

[1] P. 804.
[2] See Bailly: *Lettres sur l'Atlantide*, 1777 and *Lettres sur l'Origine des Sciences*, 1777.

[107]

Since the Hindoos and Druids are one, he feels no compunction in following a current theory, and in the *Song of Los*, we are told that

"Adam shudder'd! Noah faded! Black grew the sunny African
When Rintrah gave abstract philosophy to Brama in the East."[1]

When we read further in the same page

"To Trismegistus, Palamabron gave an abstract law
To Pythagoras, Socrates and Plato."

it requires but a little imagination (and Blake had plenty) to make Palamabron out of Parabraman, and to interpret: the Druids (Rintrah) taught the Hindoos (Brama, Parabraman) philosophy; and the Hindoos (Palamabron, Parabraman) taught it to the Egyptians (Trismegistus) and the Greeks (Pythagoras, etc.). Thus at least one more page of Blake makes sense, and we turn with relief to Sonnerat's plain statements:

"India in its splendour gave religion and laws to other nations; Egypt and Greece are indebted to the Indians both for their fables and their philosophy. Pythagoras studied in India."[2]

[1]P. 273.
[2]Sonnerat: *A voyage to the East Indies*, London, 1788, pp. i and vi Introduction.

That is what Blake had meant to say.

Of all the popular books on India, Sonnerat is the nearest to Blake's time of writing and may be taken as the most useful, and we find in Sonnerat's report of Indian religion all these essential elements of the Blakean myth:

the primitive hermaphrodite, or giant containing all the world
his separation into beings and especially
his separation into Male and Female
the refusal of the female, her flight
the pursual by the male, his conquest of the female
the origin of all species from their union.

Sonnerat reports that the Candon believe that Brama divides himself into male and female. Trismegistus derived this idea from India.[1]

Brama, thus divided, fell in love with his own daughter, called Sarassouadi. Sonnerat explains that, contrary to the opinion of fervent comparatists, she had nothing in common with Abraham's wife Sarah.[2]

Chourien is the Sun. His wife was unable to bear his ardour and leaving by his side a deluding phantom shaped like herself, took the

[1] *Ibid.* pp. 207 and 215 note and 217.
[2] *Ibid.* p. 218, pp. 9 and 72.

form of a mare and ran away. He perceived
the trick, changed into a horse, overtook her.
She conceived, and, after repeated similar
happenings, all things came from her.[1]
The *Bagavadan* (Bhagavata Purana) was published in Paris in 1789, and a similar tale is
recorded there:

Vishnou said to Brama, who had come from him:
"Cet univers et toutes les vies sont cachées dans mon
sein; je vous commande de les développer, de les
produire."[2]

So Brama produced four beings (Blake's Zoas
are four) and ordered them to create the world.
They refused. Then Brama divided his own
body into the various sorts of men.[3]
Brama also fell in love with his daughter and
won possession of her. Then he was ashamed
of himself and abandoned his body. Then the
Giants fell in love with Brama. He was pursued
by them, but, horrified, he again abandoned
his body, which became a woman whom the
Giants enjoyed. Thus Brama was sacrificed by
the Giants.[4]
In Bernier's *Voyages* (Amsterdam, 1723) we

[1]Sonnerat, p. 213.   [2]P. 63.   [3]P. 70-71.
[4]Pp. 72-78. This is also in Sonnerat, pp. 217, 218, 219.

find already a synthesis between India and the Cabala:

"Je m'en vais vous découvrir le mystère d'une grande Cabale qui a fait beaucoup de bruit ces dernières années dans l'Hindoustan. . . . Ces Cabalistes Indous prétendent que Dieu, ou Achar, a tiré de sa propre substance tout ce qu'il y a de matériel et de corporel, à la façon de l'araignée qui produit une toile.

La création donc n'est autre chose qu'une extraction et extension que Dieu fait de sa propre substance.

Ils vous diront qu'il en est de Dieu comme de la Lumière, qui est la même pour tout l'univers—mais paraît de cent façons."[1]

This is "le grand mystère de la Cabale des Yauguys."

In *Lord's discovery of the Banian religion*, we find again a long description of how Bremaw (Brama) was divided into Male and Female,[2] who marry and people the earth.

We have thus traced in books on India previous to Blake all the separate traits of this part of his mythology: the separation between male and female, spectre and emanation, their flights, pursuits, overtakings, struggles, unions and

[1]Pp. 163-166.   [2]Churchill's Collection, vol. vi. p. 311.

reproductions. But what cannot be given by references and quotations is the atmosphere of these books on India. There is a striking similarity between the incomprehensible wars of Blake's Zoas and the wars of the Hindoo Gods. No direct influence is to be thought of, but one feels as one reads that Blake was saturated with the very spirit of this mythology and has instilled his own visions with it. The mundane shell and many other shells appear in Sonnerat. Worlds are presented as eggs piled up.[1] They smash very tellingly during cosmic cataclysms.

Brouma wants to show he is equal to Chiven; just as Luvah wants to show he is the equal of Urizen. There is a great fight on the cosmic scale. Stars fall about. Vishnou comes into the fight, even as Los is apt to come into a fight between Urizen and Luvah. Vishnou has to burrow in the earth to search for the foot of a mystic column, which is God, and comes back with great difficulties. Thus Urizen explores his dens and burrows through the underworld. Brouma becomes unmovable and is cursed. Urizen is frequently petrified. Chiven is an hermaphrodite. Births, rapings, fights, genea-

[1] P. 5 and note.

logies too intricate for understanding abound in
Sonnerat and in Blake.

The Hindoo gods are struck with fear at all
these terrors and shut their eyes, even as
Blake's Eternals. They are particularly horrified
when Brama unites with his own daughter,
also as Blake's Eternals, and Brama himself is
horrified at his own deed. Thus again and
again, Urizen and Los and Luvah behave.[1]

The names even in Sonnerat are suggestive of
Blake's names: We come across Chittere-
Parouvan (p. 123), the giant Erenien, Addi
pouron (124), Aoton (130), Ouricati-Tirounal,
Ananda-Perpenadesouami (132), Paor Nomi
(138), Tirounamaley, Paeni-Caori (144), Ani
(154), Narissen (208), Allemaron (226), Amne-
monta (39), Rudden Ruddiren. In the *Bagavadan*, Emadarmen (100), Outamabaden Pra-
vetiden, Rouguen (73), Ouroucenem (334).

These can surely compare with Blake's best
such as Urizen, Enitharmon, Allamanda,
Enthuthon-Benython, Tiriel, Oothoon, Rintrah, Palamabron, etc. There is to the ear a
similarity in the use of vowels and consonants
in entirely un-English fashion, and Blake's
verbal imagination seems to me to produce

[1]Sonnerat, Pp. 5, 8, 17, 43; *Bagavadan*: passim.

births more comparable to these versions of Hindoo names than to anything else. Also the books of the Indian travellers produce the same impression of incoherence as Blake's poems. Hindoo mythologies, summarized rapidly one after the other, leave the mind somewhat puzzled, as Sonnerat and his peers sum up sect after sect without trying to make them agree one with another. This is quite legitimate in such relations. But one has the same feeling in reading Blake: the feeling of being hurried into a new mythology before one has understood the previous one. It is a possibility that from the reading of such books Blake may have caught this perturbing atmosphere and reproduced it in his own poems, aided thereto by the apparently immense ease with which he could cope with them himself.

The complete tale which Blake more or less reconstituted from the fragments quoted is given fully in the *Satapatha-Brahmana* (*Sacred Books of the East*, vol. 41).

Prajapati is the One Being, alone at first. Out of himself he produces his daughter Ushas; he falls in love with her; in horror, she flees from him; but he overtakes her and unites with her; again she flees and at each of their unions a

And there was heard a great lamenting in Beulah: all the Regions
Of Beulah were moved as the tender Bowels are moved: & they said:

Why did you take Vengeance O ye Sons of the mighty Albion?
Planting these Oaken Groves: Erecting these Dragon Temples
Injury the Lord heals but Vengeance cannot be healed:
As the Sins of Albion have done to Luvah: so they have in him
Done to the Divine Lord & Saviour. who suffers with those that suffer:
For not one sparrow can suffer, & the whole Universe not suffer also.
In all its Regions, & its Father & Saviour not pity and weep,
But Vengeance is the destroyer of Grace & Repentance in the bosom
Of the Injurer: in which the Divine Lamb is cruelly slain:
Descend O Lamb of God & take away the imputation of Sin
By the Creation of States & the deliverance of Individuals Evermore Amen

Thus wept they in Beulah over the Four Regions of Albion
But many doubted & despaird & imputed Sin & Righteousness
To Individuals & not to States, and these Slept in Ulro.

The cruel sacrifices of Albion—Adam Cadmon—Prajapati

" Man anciently contained in his mighty limbs all things in
Heaven and Earth"

(Jerusalem, p. 25)

new species of being is born of her (pp. 156-158).
Now this desire of Prajapati is a sin, and he is
punished for it by Rudra, who pierces him
(i. 208). Agni is created from his mouth (not
from a woman) (322): thus Fuzon, Urizen's
eldest born, is born before woman. Agni turns
upon Prajapati, as Fuzon upon Urizen in the
First Book.[1] Prajapati appeases him by a
sacrifice.

This same Prajapati is sacrificed by the gods
(S.B.E., iii. 1), who dismember him and make
all beings from his fragments. This is the myth
we can come to which is nearest to Blake's
cruel sacrifices creating all things from Albion.
After he is dismembered, all the divine couples
issue from him (vol. 43, p. 229), even as from
Albion come the couples Urizen-Ahania, Los-
Enitharmon, Luvah-Vala, etc.—which is a
variant of the idea that he unites with his
daughter under all the shapes of all the beings
which constitute the world.

This leads back to the celebrated hymn of the
Rig-Veda (x. 90, 7-10):

"Purusha thus born became the Sacrifice, offered
on the sacred grass by the Devas, the Sadhyas and
the Rishis.

[1]*First Book of Urizen,* viii; *Book of Ahania,* i.

[115]

From the sacrifice are born all the animals that
have a double row of teeth. . . ."

Air comes from his navel, heaven from his
head, the earth from his feet, etc. All parts of
the world, all varieties of men, all species of
beings.

Whatever the devious ways which brought this
lore to Blake, it must have come to him, as
without it one of the essential strains of his song
is incomprehensible.

From hermetism and the Cabala to theosophy
and the schools of Stanislas de Gaita[1] or
Papus[2] all the accessible systems of occultism
hold as a central doctrine the conception
of the transformation of the One into the Many
followed by the reintegration of the Many into
the One: involution and evolution, as Theosophy names it. This is obviously connected
with Plotinus' doctrine of the One, though
what the connection is history at present cannot
say. It may be that the Western world was
divided into two by the fact that the great
philosopher of the time of the Fathers was
himself no Christian, so that his ideas were
gradually driven underground to live on in

[1]*Au seuil du Mystère*, Paris, 1889.
[2]*La Cabale*, Paris, 1903.

heterodoxy. It may be that his ideas were only the purest metaphysical presentation known to us of very ancient conceptions. M. Brehier[1] holds that Plotinus derived from India the essential part of his system. Ancient Egypt had probably expressed very similar conceptions by the myth of the division and reconstitution of Osiris.

Blake, in his central doctrines, is thus one of a long and numerous tradition. His Giant Albion, divided up into beings by *cruel sacrifices* and then reconstituted and awakened from deep slumber in the Ocean, is akin to Purusha dismembered and Agni reconstituted by sacrifice; to Osiris; and to the One in Plotinus' philosophy.

And this not through extensive and profound learning on Blake's part but through the living, unbroken and yet fragmentary tradition that had come down to him.

Blake is one of the greatest occultists of all time; because he is an occultist with creative genius. He has known, obviously, many fragments of various traditions; but he has not merely repeated them or enlarged upon them; he has fused them into a whole and interpreted them into

[1] *Revue des cours et conférences*, Paris, 1922, 2ᵉ série, pp. 257, 528-531.

a large system which is alive with bold and profound ideas. As all the great masters of occultism, he has new things to say; he can look upon himself as the prophet of a new revelation.

The end of the eighteenth century is full of scattered fragments of occultism; and on a first study it might appear that it is a great occultist period. But if we try and follow the stream of occultism up the centuries, we soon realise that the late eighteenth and the early nineteenth centuries are really periods of decadence and popularisation in occultism. The greatest name is that of Swedenborg. But Swedenborg is really not a thinker at all. If there is any value in occultism, it lies in the fact that occultism keeps alive, under some prevailing official philosophy or religion, a separate tradition, an element of deep thought which has been neglected by conventional thinking. If original philosophy is absent from occultism, it becomes merely a seething mass of superstition. Judged from this point of view of philosophy (setting apart the question of truth in philosophy—a debatable thing—and insisting on originality and boldness) Swedenborg has hardly any value. His general ideas are the merest platitudes, far inferior to the Christian presentation of not very different notions. If you do not happen to believe that Swedenborg is a man who has visited heaven and hell and similar other places, and if you are not prepared to take his word as to what he saw in such places, he is of no use to you.

Blake's pronouncement over Swedenborg is perfectly accurate and well balanced. It is perhaps not sufficiently realised that Blake is a critical genius of the first order. Perhaps he is the one case in literature where criticism has risen to genius, both in expression and in thought, as, for instance, when he states that Milton "was a true poet and of the devil's party without knowing it." Of Swedenborg he says:

"Swedenborg has not written one new truth . . . he has written all the old falsehoods—Swedenborg's writings are a recapitulation of all superficial opinions and an analysis of the more sublime—but no further —Any man of mechanical talents may from the writings of Paracelsus or Jacob Boehmen, produce ten thousand volumes of equal value with Swedenborg's and from those of Dante or Shakespeare an infinite number."[1]

Barring the mathematical exaggeration of the

[1]P. 207.

ten thousand volumes, from the philosophical point of view, every word of this judgment is exact. "A man of mechanical talents," is an apt description of Swedenborg as an occultist. Blake once set apart as a man of genius, the occultists of his period are very feeble as thinkers. The great occultists in modern times belong to the seventeenth century: Robert Fludd in England, Jean d'Espagnet in France, Boehme in Germany, and later, Henry More and his German friend, Knorr von Rosenroth, lifted occultism into great and ordered philosophy. They were the antagonists or the friends of such men as Gassendi and Descartes. Compared with them, Swedenborg, Martinez de Pasqualis, de Saint Martin and later Fabre d'Olivet are very small minds. If you read them after their seventeenth century predecessors, they have nothing to teach you; they are mediocre pupils repeating fragments of an incompletely learnt lesson. You have to come, later in the nineteenth century, to Eliphas Levi and H. P. Blavatsky, to find greatness in occultism again—and yet no such clear greatness as in d'Espagnet, whose classical mind is a delight to follow, or in Boehme, who has flashes of sheer genius.

But Blake is the redeeming exception; his genius as a *knower* and a creator of occult ideas and myths is entirely unique in his period, and his contempt for Swedenborg is fully justified if we compare the two men. Of all the occultist host of the late eighteenth century, Blake alone was worthy, on the dark side of the period, of the age which produced Kant on the clear side.

Victor Hugo, who has many faults and many virtues in common with Blake, has also judged well, in *William Shakespeare*, when, after describing in his grand manner that interior abyss which every man finds in his soul:

"Qui y descend est Kant, qui y tombe est Swedenborg."

Into that abyss Kant descended with calm and brought light, Swedenborg merely fell into it and was smashed. Hugo could not know of Blake; else he would have added:

"Qui y vole est Blake."

For Blake soared down and through that abyss; only too rapid was his flight for us to follow it always.

With the mention of Kant we come to the study of Blake's idealism. For the real inheritors of the wisdom of d'Espagnet, Boehme, More and Rosenroth, were not the degenerate occultists from Martinez to Fabre d'Olivet, but the great Germans: Kant, Fichte, Hegel and Schopenhauer. The debt the German philosophers owe to the occultist thinkers will appear greater and greater as these obscure and often puzzling forerunners become better known. Blake, who continued the occultist tradition through this brilliant philosophical period, followed really on a course parallel to that of his apparently more scientific German contemporaries.

II. IDEALISM

THE senses of man create this world which surrounds us. We have already seen that they create it badly—but that is a judgment of value. Let us insist here on the fact that Man creates this world and not God. This comes to the same statement that "the Creator of this world is a very cruel being."[1] He is not the Supreme God, who is good, but at present inaccessible to us. The cruel God of this world has *bound our senses five*, and they manufacture this false cruel world. Thus Blake takes his peculiar place in his century and replaces God by man as a creator.

"How do you know but every Bird that cuts the airy
     way
Is an immense world of delight, closed by your
     senses five?

Urizen, the God of this world, through *Tirzah*
          Did bind my nostrils, eyes and ears—
          Did close my tongue in senseless clay
          And me to mortal Life betray."

[1]P. 844.

[123]

Hence:

> "The Sun's Light when he unfolds it
> Depends on the Organ that beholds it."[1]

The central idea is that everything is infinite whereas our senses make everything appear finite:

> "That there is one Omnipotent, Uncreate and God I agree, but that there is but one Infinite I do not; for if all but God is not Infinite, they shall come to an End, which God forbid."[2]

A true vision would make us "discover the infinite in everything."[3]

> "If Perceptive Organs vary, Objects of Perception seem to vary:
> If the Perceptive Organs close, their Objects seem to close also.
> 'Consider this, O mortal Man, O worm of sixty winters,' said Los,
> 'Consider Sexual Organization and hide thee in the dust.' "[4]

This power of creation of the outside world is an effect of the Fall: it works by contraction and limitation; we shall see the mechanism of it when studying the Fall in relation to the Cabala. But it is a contraction of the Divine

[1]P. 752.   [2]Pp. 935-936.   [3]P. 195.   [4]P. 616.

power: God remains in us, even in this state of fall, and still creates:

". . . Why stand we here trembling around
Calling on God for help, and not ourselves, in whom
    God dwells?"[1]

This creative power works on ourselves too and not only on the outside world. Thus Blake repeats several times the phrase, "he became what he beheld."[2] And *what he beheld* was a vision arising in himself.

"Then those in Great Eternity who contemplate on
    Death
Said thus: 'What seems to Be, Is, To those to whom
It seems to Be, and is productive of the most dreadful
Consequences to those to whom it seems to Be, even of
Torments, Despair, Eternal Death."[3]

In his notes to Berkeley's *Siris* Blake shows himself well abreast of the philosophy of his time. To Berkeley's divine idealism, he adds, on every occasion, the note *in every man,* thus bringing the creative power into the individual; and coming into line with Hume's criticism:

"Imagination of the Human Eternal Body *in Every
    Man.*"
"Imagination is the Divine Body in Every Man."

[1]P. 631.   [2]P. 467.   [3]P. 619.

"The Natural Body is an Obstruction to the Soul or
  Spiritual Body."
". . . Whence, according to Themistus, . . . it may
be inferred that all beings are in the soul. For, saith
he, the forms are the beings. By the form every
thing is what it is. And, he adds, it is the soul that
imparteth forms to matter. . . .
This is my Opinion, but Form must be apprehended
by Sense or the Eye of Imagination. Man is All
Imagination. God is Man and exists in us and we
in him."[1]

The Marriage of Heaven and Hell gives full
expression to the commandment.

> "Thy own humanity learn to adore—
> Thou art a man, God is no more."

insisting at the same time upon the falseness of
the presentation given us by our senses: they
create, but create badly:

"The cherub with his flaming sword is hereby com-
manded to leave his guard at tree of life ; and when
he does, the whole creation will be consumed and
appear infinite and holy, whereas it now appears
finite and corrupt.
This will come to pass by an improvement of sensual
enjoyment.
But first the notion that man has a body distinct

[1]Pp. 1021-1023.

from his soul is to be expunged; this I shall do by printing in the infernal method, by corrosives, which in Hell are salutary and medicinal, melting apparent surfaces away, and displaying the infinite which was hid.

If the doors of perception were cleansed every thing would appear to man as it is, infinite.

For man has closed himself up, till he sees all things thro' narrow chinks of his cavern."[1]

The three short pamphlets on Natural religion are quite as edifying on the same two points:

"I. Man cannot naturally Perceive but through his natural or bodily organs.

II. Man by his reasoning power can only compare and judge of what he has already perceiv'd.

III. From a perception of only three senses or three elements none could deduce a fourth or fifth.

IV. None could have other than natural or organic thoughts if he had none but organic perceptions.

V. Man's desires are limited by his perceptions, none can desire what he has not perceiv'd.

VI. The desires and Perceptions of man, untaught by anything but organs of sense, must be limited to objects of sense.

. . . .

VII. The desire of Man being Infinite, the possession is Infinite and himself Infinite.

[1]P. 197.

Application. He who sees the Infinite in all things, sees God. He who sees the Ratio only, sees himself only.

Therefore God becomes as we are, that we may be as he is."[1]

All this may be summed up in this terse formula of the *Marriage*:

"Some will say: Is not God alone the prolific?
I answer: God only acts and is in existing beings or Men."[2]

Thus Blake's idealistic pantheism is founded in reason, based on a critical estimate of the value of the results given us by our senses, such an estimate as has only been reached at the end of the eighteenth century in Europe.

Let us now see how this highly intellectual and modern doctrine becomes transposed into a mythology as intricate in its details as it is ancient and widespread in its connotations.

[1]Pp. 147-148.   [2]P. 198.

III. THE ONE

BLAKE knows but little about God, however frequently he may mention the name: one can make no doctrine from his references. In accordance with the occultist tradition, God is essentially to Blake unknowable: "The Deity of whom no one had any knowledge," as the gnostics said. Yet he is a personal God. Blake thus holds the same views as Milton before him and Hugo after him.

"Man can have no idea of any thing greater than Man, as a cup cannot contain more than its capaciousness. But God is a man, not because he is perceiv'd by man, but because he is the creator of man."[1]

All Beings are One Being, the Universal Man, the Adam Kadmon, Albion:

". . . a Perfect Unity
Cannot Exist but from the Universal Brotherhood
   of Eden,
The Universal Man, To Whom be Glory Evermore,
   Amen."[2]

[1]P. 934. Let us note here that this "cup" is a typical cabalistic simile. The *Zohar* says: "How would it be possible to put more water into a cup which is already filled to the brim" (de Pauly, VI., ii. 346).
[2]P. 278.

"Daughter of Beulah, Sing
His fall into Division and his resurrection to Unity."

Here we have, clearly stated, the great occultist doctrine, which is the key to the whole of Blake's thought. Blake comes back to it as frequently as he finds it useful:

"But those in Great Eternity Met in the Council of God
As one Man, hovering over Gilead and Hermon.
He is the Good Shepherd, He is the Lord and Master
To Create Man Morning by Morning, to give gifts
    at Noon day."[1]

.   .   .   .

"Eternity appeared above them as One Man."[2]

.   .   .   .

"Then those in Great Eternity met in the Council
    of God
As one Man, for contracting their Exalted Senses
They behold Multitude, or Expanding they behold
    as one,
As One Man all the Universal family; and that One
    Man
They call Jesus the Christ, and they in him and he
    in them
Live in Perfect harmony, in Eden the land of life,
Consulting as One Man above the Mountain of
    Snowdon Sublime."[3]

[1]P. 285.   [2]P. 292.
[3]P. 298, cf. 302, 398, 594, 198, 202, 765, 797.

This One Man is sometimes called Jesus—but
that is rather when he is Reconstituted, as we
have seen in explaining the poem

> "And did those feet in ancient Time
> Walk upon England's mountains green?"

Jesus is Albion reappearing.[1]
This Being, Albion-Jesus, is really only one of a
supernatural world of beings, referred to as the
Eternals. Albion seems to be the Eighth of those
beings—which brings us back to Valentine's
Ogdoad—eight Aeons:

> "But many of the Eternals rose up from eternal
>   tables
> Drunk with the Spirit; burning round the Couch of
>   death they stood
> Looking down into Beulah; wrathful, fill'd with
>   rage
> They rend the heavens round the Watchers in a fiery
>   circle
> And round the Shadowy Eighth: the Eight close up
>   the Couch
> Into a tabernacle and flee with cries down to the
>   Deeps, raging fires.
> They soon find their own place and join the Watchers
>   of the Ulro."[2]

[1]Cf. 398, 465, 466, 502, 548, 654, 663, 750, 751.
[2]P. 499.

The Shadowy Eighth, because he has fallen.
The Starry Eight are mentioned again:

"O how the Starry Eight rejoiced to see Ololon
  descended."[1]

We are given the names in *Jerusalem III* (a fairly
useless piece of information)

"Then far the greatest number were about to make
  a Separation;
And they Elected Seven, call'd the Seven Eyes of God,
Lucifer, Molech, Elohim, Shaddai, Pahad, Jehovah,
  Jesus.
They nam'd the Eighth: he came not, he hid in
  Albion's Forests."[2]

A passage which seems to imply that there are
more than eight, but that we can conceive only
of eight, and are part of only one, Albion-Adam.
Jesus here seems to be another of the Eternals
who undertook later to save Albion and thus
became Albion. Blake refers to them as being
Eight even when Albion is Fallen; and the
identification of Albion with Jesus still leaves
them Eight. They are perhaps themselves only
transitory forms of the One—and Blake does
not worry over their mathematics.[3]
These Eternals it is that were horrified at the

[1]P. 535.   [2]P. 653.
[3]Cf. 507, 548, 634, 669, 655.

works of Los and Urizen; they who praise Los
in Eternity, because he kept the divine vision
in times of trouble; they who at the end of
Jerusalem welcome Albion back to the Pleroma.
And they conversed together in visionary
forms dramatic. . . .
In the One, there is Harmony. The Eternals
are at peace. Within each Eternal all the powers
are at peace. Many allusions are made to that
state, such as the following:

"Tharmas replied: 'Art thou Urthona, My friend,
   my old companion
With whom I liv'd in happiness before that deadly night
When Urizen gave the horses of Light into the hands
   of Luvah?' "[1]

.   .   .   .

"The Spectre said: 'Thou lovely Vision, this de-
   lightful Tree
Is given us for Shelter from the tempests of Void
   and Solid,
Till once again the morn of ages shall renew upon us,
To reunite in those mild fields of happy Eternity
Where thou and I in undivided Essence walk'd about
Imbodied, thou my garden of delight and I the spirit
   in the garden;
Mutual there we dwelt in one another's joy,
   revolving

[1]P. 334, cf. 306, 321, 652, 349.

Days of Eternity, with Tharmas mild and Luvah
    sweet melodious
Upon our waters. This thou well rememberest;
    listen, I will tell
What thou forgettest. They in us and we in them
    alternate Liv'd
Drinking the joys of Universal Manhood."[1]

The Eternal who concerns us especially is
Albion: here we must distinguish between his
states, which are permanent, and the individuals which issued from him at his dismem-
berment, and which are transitory. For Blake,
the individual is a delusion, and probably each
man will wake up at the end of things to find
that he is Albion, who had fallen into the error
of thinking that he was restricted to one man.
Much in the manner in which a man's dreams
disappear on his awakening, nor are sorry to
disappear: Whatever of the man was in the
dreams subsists in the awakened man: his states.

"And thus the Seven Angels instructed him, and thus
    they converse:

'We are not Individuals but States, Combinations
    of Individuals.
We were Angels of the Divine Presence, and were
    Druids in Annandale,

[2]P. 376.

[134]

Compell'd to combine into Form by Satan, the
    Spectre of Albion,
Who made himself a God and destroyed the Human
    Form Divine.
But the Divine Humanity and Mercy gave us a
    Human Form
Because we were combin'd in Freedom and holy
    Brotherhood,
While those combin'd by Satan's Tyranny, first in
    the blood of War
And Sacrifice and next in Chains of imprisonment,
    are Shapeless Rocks.' "[1]

   .   .   .   .

" 'Descend, O Lamb of God, and take away the
    imputation of Sin
By the Creation of States and the deliverance of
    Individuals Evermore. Amen.'
Thus wept they in Beulah over the Four Regions of
    Albion;
But many doubted and despair'd and imputed Sin
    and Righteousness
To individuals and not to States, and these Slept
    in Ulro."[1]

And to the Deists Blake says:

"Rahab is an Eternal State. The Spiritual States of
the Soul are all Eternal. Distinguish between the
Man and his present State."[2]

[1]Pp. 528, 596, cf. 690.   [2]P. 646.

[135]

This puzzling line

We are not Individuals but States, Combinations of Individuals,

is probably explained most simply so as to make sense by supposing that Blake meant

We are not Individuals but States, Combinations of States,

or else by applying the second word, "Individuals," to Urizen, Los, Luvah and Tharmas, the *mighty Ones in every man,* who are States. Blake insists on the fact that no man is condemned for ever, but that some states are:

"Albion goes to Eternal Death. In Me all Eternity
Must pass thro' condemnation and awake beyond
    the Grave.
No individual can keep these Laws, for they are
    death
To every energy of man and forbid the springs of
    life.
Albion hath enter'd the State Satan! Be permanent
    O State!
And thou for ever accursed! that Albion may arise
    again.
And be thou created into a State! I go forth to
    Create
States, to deliver Individuals evermore! Amen."[1]

[1]P. 616, cf. 596, 628-629, 646.

In the general state in which we live (and this covers many secondary states) the Eternal of which we are a part, Albion, is asleep:

"Then All in Great Eternity Met in the Council of God
As one Man, Even Jesus, upon Gilead and Hermon,
Upon the Limit of Contraction to create the fallen
    Man.
The Fallen Man stretch'd like a corse upon the oozy
    Rock,
Wash'd with the tides, pale, overgrown with weeds
That mov'd with horrible dreams."[1]

We are none other than the *horrible dreams*, otherwise his *children*:

"Hoarse turn'd the Starry Wheels rending a way in
    Albion's Loins:
Beyond the Night of Beulah, In a dark and unknown
    Night:
Outstretch'd his Giant beauty on the ground in
    pain and tears:
His Children exil'd from his breast pass to and fro
    before him. . . ."[2]

It is truly a case of exclaiming with Hamlet in wonderment:

"But in that sleep of death what dreams may come."

Let us try and explore the dreams.

[1]P. 398, cf. 334, 420, 421, 490, 505.
[2]Pp. 583-585, 587, 730, 733, 742.

IV. THE FALL FROM THE ONE

WE shall find that the Fall is explained by the rebellion of Urizen, the God of this world, who *descended*. As a reason, we are given this mysterious explanation:

"Eternity groan'd and was troubled at the Image of
Eternal Death.
The Wandering Man bow'd his faint head and
Urizen descended—
And *the one must have murder'd the Man if he had not
descended*—
Indignant, muttering low thunders, Urizen descended,
Gloomy sounding: "Now I am God from Eternity
to Eternity."[1]

*And the One must have murdered the Man if he had
not descended.* This has to be interpreted, as it is
the only reason for the Fall that Blake gives us.
The only explanation I can find is the cabalistic
explanation: Evil must exist, because evil is
the difference between God and Man; if there

[1]P. 290.

[138]

were no evil, man would not exist, God would be alone. Why cannot God be alone? Because God has a certain work, only mysteriously alluded to, which can only be accomplished by individual men. Therefore he has given them individual existence, and allowed evil to be born so as to create individual men.

If Urizen had not descended from his place in the divine bosom, there would have been no Man, only the One: *the One would have murdered the Man.*

We find a long discussion in the *Zohar* on this point:

"Rabbi Simeon dit à ses collègues: . . .
'Si le Saint, béni soit-il, n'avait pas créé l'esprit du bien et l'esprit du mal, l'homme n'aurait jamais pu mériter ni démériter; . . . c'est pourquoi il est dit dans l'Écriture: Voyez, j'ai posé devant vos yeux d'un côté la Vie et le Bien; de l'autre la mort et le mal'—Les collègues répliquèrent: Pourquoi ne fallait-il que l'homme fût pourvu de l'esprit du bien seul et n'eût aucun mérite? Ainsi créé, il n'aurait jamais causé tant de ravages dans les régions célestes!"[1]

This last phrase might well apply to Urizen and his moods.

Rabbi Simeon answered that without evil there

[1]*Zohar*: trad. de Pauly, vol. i. p. 142-143.

would be no law: no law would have been necessary. But it is written:

"Dieu n'a pas créé la terre en vain, mais l'a formée afin qu'elle fût habitée."

Namely, without the law and without evil, the earth would have been empty, and the Schekhina (the Female Power in God)

"serait demeurée sans habit, à l'exemple d'un pauvre."

This is why, when two demons came to God before the creation and explained to him that He should not create men because men would do evil, the Schekhina intervened in favour of the Race that was yet to be, and persuaded God to create man, even at the cost of evil— because thus "the Schekhina would be clothed."[1]

Such is perhaps the origin of (and in any case, here is one of the texts testifying to) the idea that evil is necessary: without it, God's work would not have been done, because man would not have existed. In modern times, the cabalist tradition has been explained more clearly perhaps by Victor Hugo, who says that God necessarily created man evil :

[1] *Zohar*, de Pauly, vol. i. p. 141.

"Il le fit radieux, beau, candide, adorable,
Mais imparfait; sans quoi, sur la même hauteur,
La créature, étant égale au créateur,
Se serait avec Dieu mêlée et confondue
Et la création, à force de clarté,
En lui serait rentrée et n'aurait pas été.' "[1]

And Hugo was following Alexander Weill, a cabalist who was one of his friends and held that

"Sa force créatrice ne pouvait pas créer un être parfait ne défaillissant jamais, parce qu'elle ne pouvait créer une force égale à elle."

"Cette Essence" (si elle est parfaite) "en rentrant en lui n'est qu'une infinie partie de son tout."[2]

Hugo, trying to explain one of the aspects, and indeed the cause of evil, namely doubt, comes to the conclusion that

"Le jour où l'esprit humain ne douterait plus, l'âme humaine s'envolerait et laisserait la charrue, ayant l'aile. Votre terre resterait en friche. Or Dieu est le semeur et l'homme le laboureur. Le grain céleste commande au soc humain de rester dans le sillon."

This is strangely alike to the *Zohar's* statement that God made the Earth to be inhabited.

[1] *Les Contemplations: Ce que dit la bouche d'Ombre.*
[2] Cf. D. Saurat: *La Religion de Victor Hugo*, Introduction II.

This idea of the necessity of evil to the existence of man and therefore to the accomplishment of the work assigned by God to man is therefore a constant idea in cabalistic tradition from the thirteenth century Zohar to the nineteenth century; and since Blake knew something of the Cabala, we are justified in using this conception if it makes our text clearer.

Milton, perhaps under similar influences, had also admitted the necessity of evil.[1]

We have thus at least one surmise as to the cause of the whole *ravage* that Blake describes in the *Prophetic Books*. Let us now see what the *ravage* consists of. The Fall has many aspects. I shall try to examine the essential ones.

1. THE MANY

Let us take first the most general aspect, the neoplatonician division of the One into the Many.

> ". . . Envy, Revenge and Cruelty
> Which separated the Stars from the Mountains, the
> Mountains from Man
> And left man a little grovelling root outside of
> Himself."[2]

---

[1]Cf. D. Saurat, *Milton: Man and Thinker*, p. 133.
[2]P. 580.

That is to say, outside of the One Man, Adam-Kadmon, Albion. This general idea is a statement against jealousy, against reason, against law, against the self: all things that are *division*.

"Beyond the bounds of their own self their senses
    cannot penetrate:
As the tree knows not what is outside of its leaves
    and bark
And yet it drinks the summer joy and fears the
    winter sorrow,
So, in the regions of the grave, none knows his dark
    compeer
Tho' he partakes of his dire woes and mutual returns
    the pang,
The throb, the dolor, the convulsion, in soul-sickening
    woes."[1]

The Man being divided, each one of his parts divides: Here is one speaking:

"Los sat upon his anvil stock; they sat beside the
    forge.
Los wip'd the sweat from his red brow and thus
    began
To the delusive female forms shining among his
    furnaces:
'I am that shadowy Prophet who six thousand years
    ago
Fell from my station in the Eternal bosom. I divided

[1]Pp. 355-356, cf. 278, 288, 304, 409.

[143]

To multitude, and my multitudes are children of
　　Care and Labour
O Rahab, I behold thee. I was once like thee, a
　　Son
Of Pride, and I also have pierc'd the Lamb of God
　　in pride and wrath.
Hear me repeat my Generations that thou maist
　　also repent.' "[1]

Albion is primarily divided into four Beings,
the *Zoas*, which are many things, but which
are essentially four states, extant in every man:
Urizen is intellect, Luvah is passion, Los is
imagination, Tharmas is instinct.

The division Reason versus Passion is classical
in English literature from the Renaissance
onwards.[2]

Imagination as the source of all truth, or
Inspiration, is Blake's particular favourite
faculty. Instinct comes perhaps from the Cabala
—it does not play a very important part in
the mythology of Blake's poems.

"L'homme, dit Rabbi Yehouda, est conduit par trois
guides; par le raisonnement et la sagesse inspirés par
l'âme sainte, par la passion inspirée par le mauvais
penchant, et enfin par l'instinct de conservation

[1]P. 412.
[2]Cf. Saurat, *Milton: Man and Thinker*, p. 149 sq.

[144]

commun à tous les hommes. Remarquez que l'esprit
tentateur n'a de prise que sur les deux derniers
conducteurs. Le guide appelé passion n'attend pas
que l'esprit tentateur vienne le séduire; il court, au
contraire, au devant de lui; et c'est ce deuxième
guide qui entraîne avec lui le troisième, inoffensif
par nature."[1]

"Four Mighty Ones are in Every Man; a Perfect
  Unity
Cannot Exist but from the Universal Brotherhood of
  Eden,
The Universal Man, To Whom be Glory Evermore.
  Amen.
What are the Natures of those Living Creatures the
  Heavenly Father only
Knoweth. No Individual knoweth, nor can know in
  all Eternity.

Los was the fourth immortal starry one, and in the
  Earth
Of a bright Universe, Empery attended day and
  night,
Days and nights of revolving joy. Urthona was his
  name
In Eden; in the Auricular Nerves of Human Life,
Which is the Earth of Eden, he his Emanations
  propagated,
Fairies of Albion, afterwards Gods of the Heathen.
  Daughter of Beulah, Sing

[1]*Zohar*: vol. ii. p. 691.

His fall into Division and his Resurrection to Unity:
His fall into the Generation of decay and death, and his
Regeneration by the Resurrection from the dead.

Begin with Tharmas, Parent power, dark'ning in
    the West."[1]

Tharmas is the instinct of man, neither good
nor bad, the parent power of all man's powers.
Urizen we are sufficiently acquainted with
already. Luvah is passion: here is his first
movement, when he attempted to displace
reason, and seized the Horses of Light, the
Horses of Urizen. Which merely means that in
the state of fall passion triumphs over reason:
a sound classical doctrine, which Blake will
twist and complicate and often reverse.

"Hear! I will sing a Song of Death! it is a Song of
    Vala!
The Fallen Man takes his repose, Urizen sleeps in the
    porch,
Luvah and Vala wake and *fly* up from the Human
    Heart
Into the Brain from thence; upon the pillow Vala
    slumber'd,
And Luvah seiz'd the Horses of Light and rose into
    the Chariot of Day."[2]

[1]P. 278.
[2]P. 288—Vala is here only a part of Luvah, to become his Emanation.
(See below.)

[146]

We shall see that this deed, the triumph of passion, is probably the prime cause of Man's fall, even as it is in Milton.[1]

We have just quoted, as an example of the further sub-divisions of Man once fallen, Los's introductory speech about himself as the Shadowy Prophet.[2]

These Four Powers, in Heaven, lived in harmony and unity, as we have seen; once fallen into division each fights the others for preeminence. The end of the First Canto of *Vala* gives a long and magnificent description of how messengers came to the Eternals and told them of War broken out within Albion:

"For messengers from Beulah come in tears and
    dark'ning clouds
Saying, 'Shiloh is in ruins, our brother is sick:
    Albion, He
Whom thou lovest, is sick; he wanders, from his house
    of Eternity.
The Daughters of Beulah, terrified, have clos'd the
    Gate of the Tongue.
Luvah and Urizen contend in war around the holy
    tent.'

[1] Cf. 299-302, 291, 305-6, 320-321.
[2] Cf. on Los: 234, 236, 240, 289, 248, 290.

[147]

So spoke the Ambassadors from Beulah, and with
    solemn mourning
They were introduc'd to the divine presence, and
    they kneeled down
In Conway's Vale, thus recounting the Wars of
    Death Eternal:

The Eternal Man wept in the holy tent: Our Brother
    in Eternity,
Even Albion whom thou lovest,wept in pain; his family
Slept round on hills and valleys in the regions of his
    love.
But Urizen awoke, and Luvah woke, and they
    conferr'd."[1]

It is impossible to quote the descriptions of all
the battles: that would be quoting the whole
of the *Prophetic Books*. Let us listen only to each
power's affirmation of his own supremacy.
Los and Tharmas:

" 'And Los remains God over all, weak father of
    worms and clay.
I know I was Urthona, keeper of the gates of heaven,
But now I am all powerful Los, and Urthona is but
    my shadow.'

Doubting stood Tharmas in the solemn darkness;
    his dim Eyes
Swam in red tears; he rear'd his waves above the
    head of Los

[1]Pp. 298 sq., 332-333, 375, and passion.

[148]

In wrath, but pitying back withdrew with many a sigh.
Now he resolv'd to destroy Los, and now his tears
    flow'd down.

In scorn stood Los, red sparks of blighting from his
    furious head
Flew over the waves of Tharmas; pitying, Tharmas
    stayed his Waves,
For Enitharmon shriek'd amain, crying: 'O my
    sweet world
Built by the Architect divine, whose love to Los and
    Enitharmon
Thou rash abhorred Demon in thy fury hast o'er-
    thrown!'
'What Sovereign Architect,' said Tharmas, 'dare my
    will controll?
For if I will, I urge these waters. If I will, they sleep
In peace beneath my awful frown; my will shall be
    my Law.' "[1]

Tharmas again:

" 'Now all comes into the power of Tharmas. Urizen
    is fall'n
And Luvah hidden in the Elemental forms of Life
    and Death.
Urthona is My Son. O Los, thou art Urthona, and
    Tharmas
Is God. The Eternal Man is seal'd, never to be
    deliver'd.

[1]P. 331.

I roll my floods over his body, my billows and waves
    pass over him,
The sea encompasses him and monsters of the deep
    are his companions.
Dreamer of furious oceans, cold sleeper of weeds and
    shells,
Thy Eternal form shall never renew, my uncertain
    prevails against thee.' "[1]

Luvah:

" 'And Luvah strove to gain dominion over *mighty*
    Albion.
They strove together above the Body where Vala
    was inclos'd
And the dark Body of *Albion* left prostrate upon the
    crystal pavement,
Cover'd with boils from head to foot, the terrible
    smitings of Luvah.' "[2]

As for Urizen, we know him well already:

" 'Am I not God?' said Urizen. 'Who is Equal to
    me?
Do I not stretch the heavens abroad, or fold them up
    like a garment?'
He spoke, mustering his heavy clouds around him,
    black, opake.
Then thunders roll'd around and lightnings darted
    to and fro;

[1]Pp. 334-335, cf. 354, 363.   [2]P.323.

His visage chang'd to darkness, and his strong right
    hand came forth
To cast Ahania to the Earth."[1]

Thus the Wars of the Zoas begin. This first process of dissension is accompanied by a process of contraction. Each power of man becomes smaller when separated from the other powers.

2. CONTRACTION AND EXPANSION

Professor B. Fehr has first pointed out (in *Englische Studien*, 1920) that Blake makes use of a good deal of the machinery of the Cabala, especially shells and garments, and has suggested Rosenroth as a possible means of contact.

Here we have tried to enlarge the problem and show that the general spirit of Blake's system is the spirit of the Cabala, or of that wider occultism, of which the Cabala serves as the best witness. But there is no doubt that the nearly technical machinery of the Cabala is easily recognized in Blake's poems, particularly in this theory of Contraction as the Fall and the Creation. The theory of *retraction* is the most

[1]P. 324.

characteristic of the Cabalistic theories. As God is everything, in order to make room for the Creation, he has had to retract. This retraction (Zimzoum) has made the world, in the part of himself thus freed from His own will. The idea of retraction and contraction can then be applied to every creative process. The *Tikhoune Zohar* says:

"Quand on songe que le Saint, béni soit-il, est infini et qu'il remplit tout on comprend aisément que toute idée de création eût été impossible sans le *zimzoum* (retrait). Comment, en effet, introduire de l'eau dans une coupe déjà pleine jusqu'aux bords? Le Saint, béni soit-il, a donc resserré la Sainte Lumière qui constitue son essence; non pas qu'il se soit rapetissé—que Dieu nous préserve d'une telle opinion;—Dieu étant le tout, il ne peut ni grandir ni diminuer. Seulement, comme la lumière de Dieu est d'une telle pureté et d'un tel éclat qu'elle éclipse tout, même les anges supérieurs, même les Hayoth, même les Séraphim et les Chéroubim, le Saint, béni soit-il, pour rendre l'existence des mondes célestes et des mondes matériels possible, a retiré sa lumière puissante d'une partie de soi-même."

Blake has a precise statement to much the same effect:

"We live as One Man, for contracting our infinite
  senses
We behold multitude, or expanding we behold as one,
As One Man all the Universal family."[1]

Multitude is created by a *contraction* of the
Creator's senses, which then cease to perceive
him as One.
This idea of contraction Blake applies every-
where: Our senses are limited:

"I. Man cannot naturally Perceive but through
   his natural or bodily organs.

II. Man by his reasoning power can only compare
   and judge of what he has already perceiv'd.

III. From a perception of only three senses or three
   elements none could deduce a fourth or fifth.

IV. None could have other than natural or organic
   thoughts if he had none but organic perceptions.

V. Man's desires are limited by his perceptions,
   none can desire what he has not perceiv'd.

VI. The desires and perceptions of man, untaught
   by any thing but organs of sense, must be
   limited to objects of sense."

· · · · · · · ·

VII. The desire of Man being Infinite, the possession
   is Infinite and himself Infinite.

Application. He who sees the Infinite in all things,

[1] P. 620, cf. 583-587, 629, 645.

sees God. He who sees the Ratio only, sees himself only.

Therefore God becomes as we are, that we may be as he is."[1]

In *The Marriage of Heaven and Hell*, every Bird

Is an immense world of delight, closed by our senses five.

Our feelings and actions are similarly limited. Throughout the *First Book of Urizen*, Orc is bound with chain on chain,[2] a process which is repeated in *Vala*[3]; this represents the beginning of Jealousy: Los is jealous of Orc's love for Enitharmon. Feeling ought to remain universal and undivided; jealousy contracts to one person, and casts out every one else from participation. Jealousy is thus condemned by Blake, as we have already seen, as a principle of limitation, individuation, contraction.

". . . such is that false
And Generating Love, a pretence of love to destroy
    love,
Cruel hipocrisy, unlike the lovely delusions of
    Beulah,
And cruel forms, unlike the merciful forms of
    Beulah's Night.

[1]Pp. 147, 148, cf. 200, 237.
[2]Chapter VII.   [3]Pp. 345-348.

[154]

They know not why they love nor wherefore they
    sicken and die,
Calling that Holy Love which is Envy, Revenge and
    Cruelty,
Which separated the stars from the mountains, the
    mountains from Man
And left Man, a little grovelling Root outside of
    Himself."[1]

Morality is similarly a contraction and a
limitation—and to be similarly condemned.

"Those who restrain desire, do so because theirs is
weak enough to be restrained; and the restrainer or
reason usurps its place and governs the unwilling.
And being restrain'd, it by degrees becomes passive,
till it is only the shadow of desire."[2]

We must note that the condemnation that
Blake invariably attaches to the process is not
at all in the spirit of the Cabala: Blake takes
the technical machinery from the Cabalists,
but his judgment is the gnostic judgment, as we
have seen: the Creation is a fall, because the
Creator was an inferior or evil Demiurge.
Blake hardly ever attaches himself to one school
of thought, but mixes many shades together in

[1]P. 580, cf. 206 sq., 226, 239, 283, and, on female jealousy: 279, 284,
310, 330.
[2]P. 191.

his attempt at expressing his own very complicated thought.

Much of Blake's material machinery is derived from the Cabala. Professor Fehr has rightly insisted, in his article in *Englische Studien*, on the *shells* in Blake and shown their presence in Rosenroth. We have seen that *shells* and *mundane eggs* also came from India. Now many other technical terms of a similar metaphorical technicality are used by Blake. The attempt to trace and explain them all is of little use, because Blake does not use them consistently. He no doubt helped himself abundantly from the Cabala and other systems, but he cared little what use he made of what he had adopted. All we can do is to point out that he has adopted the terms; that he has used them both recklessly and fancifully, and added to them similar terms of his own when he listed, any persevering reader of the *Prophetic Books* will confess.

For instance, we find in the *Zohar* a whole system of the metaphysics of light; light is the substance of God, and by becoming *contracted* or *obscured*, produces all varieties of matter. A pantheistic materialism is based on this theory.[1]

[1]Cf. D. Saurat. *Milton et le matérialisme chrétien* (Rieder), Passim.

Blake evidently knows of this theory, but he makes no consistent use of it at all. Only the theory enables us to understand his passing references to Light.[1]

His lovely passage on the windows is also a cabalistic idea which he toys with and then drops:

"Five windows light the cavern'd Man: thro' one he
    breathes the air;
Thro' one hears music of the spheres; thro' one the
    eternal vine
Flourishes, that he may receive the grapes; thro' one
    can look
And see small portions of the eternal world that ever
    groweth;
Thro' one himself pass out what time he please; but
    he will not,
For stolen joys are sweet and bread eaten in secret
    pleasant."[2]

Thus in the *Zohar*, Man's brain is surrounded by shells (vol. i. pp. 119, 130, 137, de Pauly) but the shells have cracks which let the divine light come in and are men's senses.[3]

[1] Pp. 350, 354, 428, 447-448, 532, 616, 698, 941.

[2] P. 233.

[3] Professor Fehr has given the quotation from Rosenroth, i. 31: Quae quasi fenestrae sunt; vocantur in illo aures, oculi, nasus et os. (*Engli. St.* 1920.)

We shall here therefore merely tabulate some of the expressions of that order used by Blake:

Shells: 303, 312, 492, 532, 535, 539, 600-1, 660.
Egg: 513, 532-533, 572, 696, 702, 720, 740.
Windows: 232, 290, 291 (cf. also Zohar, v. III. p. 433: where immorality dirties the windows).
Tent that cuts Man off from Heaven: 252 sq. (Zohar, vol. iv. p. 317).
Light: 350, 354, 428, 447-448, 523, 616, 698, 941 cold[1]: 601, 620.
The two Suns, one dead and one living (Swedenborg and Cabala): 937.[2]
The two forces: centrifugal and centripetal[1]: the Prolific and the Devourer: 191-198.
Limits (gnostic: Oros):[3] 340, 381, 398, 401.
Vortexes: 359, 360, 490, 641; Wheels: 427, 634-635 (Zohar, iv. p. 261-277 and v., vi. notes p. 182.)
Polypus: 534, 536, 574, 583, 643, 680, 683.

3. PASSION AND SEX

The result of the fall being division and chaos in man, Blake insists particularly on the sexual aspect of this division. We shall see presently how Man became male and female. Let us

---

[1]Cf. Fludd—quoted in Saurat: *Milton et le matérialisme chrétien*, p. 26.
[2]Cf. Hugo: cet affreux soleil noir d'où rayonne la nuit. (*Bouche d'Ombre.*) See Saurat: *La Religion de Victor Hugo.*
[3]See above, part i.

[158]

first insist on passion, and specially sexual
passion, which is the cause of the division. It is
true that Urizen is blamed for the existence of
the world, but Urizen, Intellect, was called in
and allowed to rule because Luvah, passion,
had rebelled and utter confusion was feared.
And this happened because Albion had a sexual
dream. The first fall of all was sexual desire:

> "One dread morn—
> Listen, O vision of Delight! One dread morn of
> goary blood
> The manhood was divided, for the gentle passions,
> making way
> Thro' the infinite labyrinths of the heart and thro'
> the nostrils issuing
> In odorous stupefaction, stood before the Eyes of
> Man
> A female bright. I stood beside my anvil dark, a
> mass
> Of iron glow'd bright prepar'd for spade and plow-
> shares: sudden down
> I sunk with cries of blood issuing downward in the
> veins
> Which now my rivers were become, rolling in tube-
> like forms
> Shut up within themselves descending down. I sunk
> along
> The goary tide even to the place of seed, and there
> dividing

I was divided in darkness and oblivion; thou an
    infant woe,
And I an infant terror in the womb of Enion.''[1]

It was even thus that the Hindoo giant desired
the female bright that had issued from him.

            "... now listen, I will tell
Thee Secrets of Eternity which ne'er before unlock'd
My golden lips nor took the bar from Enitharmon's
    breast.
Among the Flowers of Beulah walk'd the Eternal
    Man and saw
Vala, the lily of the desert melting in high noon;
Upon her bosom in sweet bliss he fainted. Wonder
    seiz'd
All heaven; they saw him dark; they built a golden
    wall
Round Beulah. There he revel'd in delight among the
    Flowers.
Vala was pregnant and brought forth Urizen, Prince
    of Light,
First born of Generation. Then behold a wonder to
    the Eyes
Of the now fallen Man; a double form Vala appear'd
    a Male
And female; shudd'ring pale the Fallen Man
    recoil'd
From the Enormity and call'd them Luvah and Vala,
    turning down

             [1]Pp. 376-377.

The vales to find his way back into Heaven, but
    found none,
For his frail eyes were faded and his ears heavy and
    dull.
Urizen grew up in the plains of Beulah. Many sons
And many daughters flourish'd round the holy Tent
    of Man
Till he forgot Eternity, delighted in his sweet joy
Among his family, his flocks and herds and tents and
    pastures."[1]

This was the Fall: Albion went to Vala. Even
so in the Cabala, Adam went to Lilith. Now,
even as Adam had Eve for a wife, Albion had
Jerusalem as his emanation. We can try here
to draw a difficult distinction. Blake, as we have
seen, is a strong panegyrist of sex and a con-
demner of jealousy. Why then was Albion's act,
in going to Vala and not to Jerusalem, a fall?
Jerusalem represents in Albion the total
feminity; even as Albion is all men, Jerusalem
is, in him, all women: the Schekhina of the
Cabalists, the Female power in God.
Vala is only Luvah's emanation—and Luvah
is passion. Vala is passion individualised.
Man errs when he loves *one* woman: his love
for woman should be general and not individualised. Thus we come again upon Blake's

[1]P. 375.

[161]

reversed distinction between right and wrong in sex: <u>Sexual love is right when it goes to all women indistinctly; it is wrong when it concentrates upon *one*.</u>[1]

The Fall took place when Man individualised his passion. Such is the meaning of the *female bright* in the previous passages. Thus sexual passion, arising in the First Undivided being, separated from him a *female bright*, which he desired to possess. Thus division between individual male and female was brought about.

"Man is adjoin'd to Man by his Emanative portion
Who is Jerusalem in every individual Man, and her
Shadow is Vala, builded by the Reasoning power in
    Man.
O search and see: turn your eyes upward: open, O
    thou World
Of Love and Harmony in Man: expand thy ever
    lovely Gates!"[2]

Vala has brought about the division and later she is called

"Vala, the Wife of Albion, who is the daughter of Luvah."[3]

She is the daughter of Luvah (Passion) because

[1]See above: Part i., cf. 568: Vala is the Shadow of Jerusalem, 609, 614, 618.
[2]P. 636, cf. 664.   [3]P. 670.

she is his emanation, and in the state of innocence she is not to be separated from him. But
in the state of Fall, she becomes Albion's wife,
which is wrong.

Therefore, Jerusalem, the rightful wife of
Albion, laments herself:

"At length he sat on London Stone and heard
    Jerusalem's voice:

'Albion, I cannot be thy Wife; thine own Minute
    Particulars
Belong to God alone, and all thy little ones are holy;
They are of Faith and not of Demonstration; where-
    fore is Vala
Cloth'd in black mourning upon my river's currents?
    Vala awake!
I hear thy shuttles sing in the sky, and round my
    limbs
I feel the iron threads of love and jealousy and
    despair.'

Vala reply'd: 'Albion is mine! Luvah gave me to
    Albion
And now receives reproach and hate. Was it not said
    of old,
—Set your Son before a man and he shall take you
    and your sons
For slaves; but set your Daughter before a man and She
Shall make him and his sons and daughters your
    slaves for ever?—

[163]

And is this Faith? Behold the strife of Albion and
    Luvah
Is great in the east, their spears of blood rage in the
    eastern heaven.
Urizen is champion of Albion; they will slay my
    Luvah,
And thou, O harlot daughter, daughter of despair,
    art all
This cause of these shakings of my towers on
    Euphrates.
Here is the House of Albion and here is thy secluded
    place,
And here we have found thy sins; and hence we turn
    thee forth
For all to avoid thee, to be astonish'd at thee for thy
    sins,
Because thou art the impurity and the harlot, and
    thy children,
Children of whoredoms, born for Sacrifice, for the
    meat and drink
Offering, to sustain the glorious combat and the
    battle and war,
That Man may be purified by the death of thy
    delusions.' "[1]

A telling passage. Urizen is the champion of
Albion and Luvah will be killed: passion having
broken loose, Reason has been called upon to
control it. Urizen has been given power and

[1]Pp. 609-610.

[164]

he will create this logical, terrible world to imprison Luvah. Vala laments this, and calls Jerusalem a harlot. Vala speaks with the voice and the morality of this world; to her, the love of Jerusalem, the indiscriminate love of all women (advocated by Blake as tending to the ideal of Unity, as with some gnostics) is harlotry. . . .

All this is figuratively expressed by Luvah seizing the horses of Urizen *that dread morn,* which is the beginning of the ravages.

"Beyond this Universal Confusion, beyond the
    remotest Pole
Where their vortexes began to operate, there stands
A Horrible rock far in the South; it was forsaken
    when
Urizen gave the horses of Light into the hands of
    Luvah.
On this rock lay the faded head of the Eternal Man
Enwrapped round with weeds of death, pale cold in
    sorrow and woe."[1]

And Urizen is asked:

"Why didst thou listen to the voice of Luvah that
    dread morn
To give the immortal steeds of light to his deceitful
    hands?

[1] P. 427.

[165]

No longer now obedient to thy will, thou art compell'd
To forge the curbs of iron and brass, to build the iron
    mangers,
To feed them with intoxication from the wine
    presses of Luvah
Till the Divine Vision and Fruition is quite
    obliterated."[1]

Thus mankind fell into Sex: into a Feminine
Tabernacle: men had to be born of women,
and then to love and worship women:

"What may Man be? who can tell! but what may
    Woman be
To have power over Man from Cradle to corruptible
    Grave?
There is a Throne in every Man, it is the Throne of
    God;
This, Woman has claim'd as her own, and Man is
    no more!
Albion is the Tabernacle of Vala and her Temple,
And not the Tabernacle and Temple of the Most
    High.
O Albion, why wilt thou Create a Female Will?
To hide the most evident God in a hidden covert, even
In the shadows of a Woman and a secluded Holy
    Place,
That we may pry after him as after a stolen treasure,
Hidden among the Dead and mured up from the
    paths of life."[2]

[1]P. 321   [2]Pp. 614-615.

But we shall see that sex must vanish in the reconstitution of the One. Sex has no permanent value for Blake as a separate power. It is a part of every being. This may perhaps serve to attenuate the theoretical seeming immorality of his proposal of universal sexual love.

4. MALE AND FEMALE

The next aspect of the fall is therefore the division of man into sexes. Here again we come to the same relationship between Blake and the Cabala. The Cabala tells us of Man's division into Male and Female, but finds it a good thing. Blake follows cabalistic precedent, but his judgment of value is different.

The *Zohar* teaches us that Adam was originally one; and that God divided him into two beings, one male and one female. This was because God himself contains a feminine power, the Matrona or Schekhina and by sexual union with her, produces the world, which is her child. Therefore all beings are, in themselves, at once male and female, before being divided up into one male and one female. These two parts of the same soul have to be re-united before things are set right; and thus each

[167]

earthly being has its twin soul in the opposite sex. Much of the trouble of the world is caused by the search of the twin souls for each other, the errors and fights that ensue.[1]

It is easy to follow this myth throughout the prophetic books. Each of the Zoas is divided into male and female. Thus we have the four couples: Urizen and Ahania, Los and Enitharmon, Luvah and Vala, Tharmas and Enion.

Their separation is the beginning of the tumult.[2] It takes place, even as it does in the *Zohar*, by a sharp material division; the cutting into two parts, male and female, of the body of the previous being.

Thus Fuzon cuts Urizen into two, and Ahania is created: *Book of Ahania*, ch. i.

Thus, through pity, Los is divided physically into two, and Enitharmon appears: *First Book of Urizen*, ch. v.

Immediately the Males thus produced desire to embrace the corresponding females. This is a cabalistic law, which Milton applied to his picture of Satan and his daughter Sin:

Karppe, in his *Etude sur le Zohar* (p. 427) notes

[1] I have assembled the *Zohar* texts covering this myth in *La littérature et l'occultisme*. (Paris, Rieder.)

[2] Cf. 260, 300, 252, 310, 325, 328-329, 335, 375-377, 381, 650, 554, 558.

The division of Los into Male and Female : Enitharmon is created

(The First Book of Urizen, ch. v)

(B.M. colour prints by Blake, plate 19)

that: "it is a law found over and again relating to the Sephiroth . . . the female first issues from the male and then is fecundated by him." Thus, Vala, as we have seen, is called the daughter of Luvah. Thus, to go further East, Brama wishes to possess his daughter.

The reference to the Hindoos is apposite, because here Blake brings in another myth and another meaning: for the Cabala, there can be nothing wrong in sexual intercourse, a sacred thing when surrounded by the proper religious observances. But we have seen that in India, the deed of Brama or Prajapati aroused the horror of the Gods, even as in Blake:

> "Eternity shuddered when they saw
> Man begetting his likeness
> On his own divided image."[1]

It aroused the horror of the female herself, who flees from the consummation. So, all through the prophetic books, confusion is wrought by the flight of the female:

> "He embraced her; she wept, she refused;
> In perverse and cruel delight
> She fled from his arms, yet he followed."[2]

[1]P. 253.
[2]P. 253, cf. 264, 286, 302, 310, 311, 314-315, 317.

This gives rise to hatred: the deep hatred which is for Blake the solid half of love:

"The joy of woman is the death of her most beloved
Who dies for Love of her
In torments of fierce jealousy and pangs of adoration.
The Lovers' night bears on my song
And the nine spheres rejoice beneath my powerful
    controll."[1]

for woman wants power too, even as each separate Zoa wanted power over man: every part individualised by the evil division of the fall wants complete control. Hence the frequent reign of woman, her usurpation of sovereignty, which is one of the worst conditions of existence in this world. Enitharmon, separated, sings:

"Now comes the night of Enitharmon's joy!
Who shall I call? Who shall I send,
That Woman, lovely Woman, may have dominion?
Arise, O Rintrah, thee I call! and Palamabron, thee!
Go! tell the Human race that Woman's love is Sin;
That an Eternal life awaits the worms of sixty
    winters
In an allegorical abode where existence hath never
    come.
Forbid all Joy, and from her childhood shall the
    little female
Spread nets in every secret path."[2]

[1] P. 316.   [2] P. 235, cf. 239, 729-735.

[170]

Yet woman also is unhappy, apart from Man, and the *Prophetic Books* are full of the lamentation of the Females, the Emanations, wailing over the Separations:

"The lamenting voice of Ahania
Weeping upon the void!
And round the Tree of Fuzon,
Distant in solitary night,
Her voice was heard, but no form
Had she; but her tears from clouds
Eternal fell round the Tree.

And the voice cried: 'Ah, Urizen! Love!
Flower of morning! I weep on the verge
Of Non-entity; how wide the Abyss
Between Ahania and thee!

I lie on the verge of the deep;
I see thy dark clouds ascend;
I see thy black forests and floods,
A horrible waste to my eyes!' "

.   .   .   .

"Where is my golden palace?
Where my ivory bed?
Where the joy of my morning hour?
Where the sons of eternity singing

To awake bright Urizen, my king,
To arise to the mountain sport,
To the bliss of eternal valleys;

[171]

To awake my king in the morn,
To embrace Ahania's joy
On the breadth of his open bosom?
From my soft cloud of dew to fall
In showers of life on his harvests,

When he gave my happy soul
To the sons of eternal joy,
When he took the daughters of life
Into my chambers of love."[1]

5. EMANATION AND SPECTRE

Blake complicates this fairly simple and human myth by connecting it with his attack upon Abstract Reason. The Male and Female division is so to speak lined with the Spectre and Emanation division. Essentially, the Spectre is the Male and the Emanation the Female. Hard logical abstract intellect goes with the male; soft delusion, dreamy and comforting, goes with the female. Each quality, when separated, becomes exaggerated and leads to catastrophe. This represents rather in Blake another cabalistic dichotomy: in God there is the side of Rigour and the side of Pity[2]. The side of Rigour is connected with the Male and the side of Pity

[1]Pp. 264, 265, cf. 552, 556, 567, 587, 636, 747.
[2]*Zohar*, vol. v. pp. 366, 367.

[172]

His Spectre driven by the Starry Wheels of Albions sons. black and
Opake divided from his back: he labours and he mourns!

For as his Emanation divided, his Spectre also divided
In terror of those starry wheels; and the Spectre stood over Los
Howling in pain: a blackning Shadow, blackning dark & opake
Cursing the terrible Los: bitterly cursing him for his friendship
To Albion, suggesting murderous thoughts against Albion.

Los rag'd and stamp'd the earth in his might & terrible wrath!
He stood and stamp'd the earth; then he threw down his hammer in rage &
In fury; then he sat down and wept, terrified! Then arose
And chaunted his song, labouring with the tongs and hammer:
But still the Spectre divided, and still his pain increas'd!

In pain the Spectre divided: in pain of hunger and thirst
To devour Los's Human Perfection, but when he saw that Los

Los and his Spectre

(*Jerusalem*, p. 6)

with the Female. We have seen already how the Matrona, who is, in God, the side of Pity, the Female, pleaded that man should be given existence, in spite of his sins.

This does not quite coincide with the division Male and Female. One of the chief themes of *Jerusalem* is the fight between Los and his Spectre. This is figurative of all struggles for regeneration, for Los is Imagination, and it is when Imagination shall have subdued its spectre, hard abstraction, that mankind will be regenerated. Hence the well known inscription in the engraving on page 41 of *Jerusalem*:

> "Each Man is in his Spectre's power
> Until the arrival of that hour
> When his humanity awake
> And cast his Spectre into the lake."

Blake thus connects this Side of Rigour with the reasoning intellect.

> "The Spectre is the Reasoning Power in Man, and
> when separated
> From Imagination and closing itself as in steel in a Ratio
> Of the Things of Memory, it thence frames Laws
> and Moralities
> To destroy ˌImagination, the Divine Body, by
> Martyrdoms and Wars."[1]

[1]P. 699, cf. 248, 377, 598, 619, 578-579, 651, 562, 600.

[173]

It is the presence of this harsh power, at enmity with everything gentle, which further complicates matters in the sexual life: we have seen that the Female fled and was chased by the Male. But when the Spectre dominates in the Male, it drives the female furiously away, and refuses to have anything to do with her. Then the Female, female-like, tries to cling to the Male, whereas in the other situation when the Male desires her, she flees. This clears many apparent contradictions in Blake. Urizen, who is essentially a Spectral power, drives his emanation, Ahania, away, very early in the tale, and Ahania laments in vain for a long time:

> "But now alone over rocks, mountains,
> Cast out from thy lovely bosom,
> Cruel jealousy! selfish fear!
> Self-destroying, how can delight
> Renew in these chains of darkness,
> Where bones of beasts are strewn
> On the bleak and snowy mountains,
> Where bones from the birth are buried
> Before they see the light?"[1]

This is yet another aspect of the fight for power among the divided parts of the soul. The

[1]P. 266, cf. 552, 567, 560, 587, 636, 747.

Spectre drives the emanation away, or, reversely, tries to capture her in order to imprison her and torture her, in order to have complete power over man.

It is useful to note that whereas there is a distinction between the Male and the Spectre, and Los can fight his Spectre, there is no similar distinction between the Female and the Emanation. The Female is the Emanation: the feminine twin part of each soul. The Spectre is really a non-existent phantom which arises in Man, one of those States that shall be utterly destroyed (into the lake).

Blake tells us precisely that the Spectre has no Emanation.

"For a Spectre has no emanation but what he
    imbibes from deceiving
A Victim."[1]

A Man cannot be re-united to his Wife, a Being to his Emanation until he has subdued the Spectre.

"For Los said: 'Tho' my Spectre is divided, as I am
    a Living Man
I must compell him to obey me wholly, that
    Enitharmon may not
Be lost, and lest he should devour Enitharmon. Ah me!

[1]P. 677.

[175]

Piteous image of my soft desires and loves, O
    Enitharmon!
I will compell my Spectre to obey."[1]

It is useful to note that the Universal Spectre
is Satan,[2] and that Satan is Urizen in his
Spectral Mood. The Chaos of Blake's *Prophetic
Books* is thus chiefly made up of the mingling of
these various themes:

The fall of the One into multiplicity and indivi-
duality;

The division of the one into four Zoas and their
struggles for power;

The division of each being into male and female and
the pursuit of the female by the male, with the
births and rebirths attendant thereto;

The division of each being into Spectre and Emanation, the Spectre not exactly covering the Male; the
struggle between the Spectre and the being it tyran-
nizes over; the sufferings of the Emanations driven
away or tortured by the Spectres.

This chaos of disintegration is being made
more chaotic still by the attempts at reconstitution which are simultaneously being carried
on by the Powers with the help of the Eternals.
We must now examine this process of Salvation.

[1]P. 579.   [2]P. 598.

V. SALVATION: THE RECONSTITUTION OF THE ONE

SALVATION is the complicated process which undoes the work done by all the elements we have so far studied. Complicated it necessarily is, since each one of the wheels must be made to turn backwards, but the whole process of Salvation rests on two points, or two aspects of the same point:

The regeneration of passion;
The suppression of individual self.

Passion fundamentally caused the Fall, because it brought about Urizen's power as a remedy and his consequent evil creation. In Blake's mythology, the process runs thus:

Albion has been subdued by Vala,
Luvah, left without emanation by this sinful union, has had to be reborn as Orc from Los and Enitharmon—which merely means that passion must be regenerated by imagination before it becomes acceptable—Los being imagination. But Los, frightened at Orc's violence, has imprisoned him.

[177]

The moral problem is the freeing of Passion from the bonds of Imagination (an imprisonment which has yet been necessary for Passion). The mythological problem before Blake is therefore: how to free Orc, and how to unite him again to Vala. On this turns the whole history of the world.

Blake here has played fair and given this event due pre-eminence: he has devoted to it the magnificent *Preludium* to America. Let us remember that the shadowy daughter of Urthona (Los) is Vala, also reborn from Los, and that Orc is Luvah reborn, refound by Vala after separation, sin and evil:

PRELUDIUM

"The shadowy Daughter of Urthona stood before red Orc,
When fourteen suns had faintly journey'd o'er his dark abode;
His food she brought in iron baskets, his drink in cups of iron:
Crown'd with a helmet and dark hair the nameless female stood;
A quiver with its burning stores, a bow like that of night,
When pestilence is shot from heaven: no other arms she need!

[178]

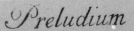

Preludium

The shadowy daughter of Urthona stood before red Orc.
When fourteen suns had faintly journey'd o'er his dark abode;
His food she brought in iron baskets, his drink in cups of iron;
Crown'd with a helmet & dark hair the nameless female stood;
A quiver with its burning stores, a bow like that of night,
When pestilence is shot from heaven; no other arms she need:
Invulnerable tho' naked, save where clouds roll round her loins,
Their awful folds in the dark air; silent she stood as night;
For never from her iron tongue could voice or sound arise;
But dumb till that dread day when Orc assay'd his fierce embrace.

Dark virgin; said the hairy youth, thy father stern abhorr'd;
Rivet my tenfold chains while still on high my spirit soars;
Sometimes an eagle screaming in the sky, sometimes a lion,
Stalking upon the mountains, & sometimes a whale I lash
The raging fathomless abyss, anon a serpent folding
Around the pillars of Urthona, and round thy dark limbs,
On the Canadian wilds I fold, feeble my spirit folds.
For chain'd beneath I rend these caverns; when thou bringest food
I howl my joy; and my red eyes seek to behold thy face
In vain! these clouds roll to & fro, & hide thee from my sight.

Invulnerable tho' naked, save where clouds roll
    round her loins
Their awful folds in the dark air: silent she stood as
    night;
For never from her iron tongue could voice or sound
    arise,
But dumb till that dread day when Orc assay'd his
    fierce embrace.
'Dark Virgin,' said the hairy youth, 'thy father
    stern, abhorr'd,
Rivets my tenfold chains while still on high my
    spirit soars;
Sometimes an eagle screaming in the sky, sometimes
    a lion
Stalking upon the mountains, and sometimes a
    whale, I lash
The raging fathomless abyss; anon a serpent folding
Around the pillars of Urthona, and round thy dark
    limbs
On the Canadian wilds I fold; feeble my spirit
    folds,
For chain'd beneath I rend these caverns: when
    thou bringest food
I howl my joy, and my red eyes seek to behold thy
    face—
In vain! these clouds roll to and fro, and hide thee
    from my sight.'

Silent as despairing love, and strong as jealousy,
The hairy shoulders rend the links; free are the
    wrists of fire;

Round the terrific loins he seiz'd the panting,
    struggling womb;
It joy'd: she put aside her clouds and smiled her
    first-born smile,
As when a black cloud shows its lightnings to the
    silent deep.
Soon as she saw the terrible boy, then burst the
    virgin cry:
'I know thee, I have found thee, and I will not let
    thee go:
Thou art the image of God who dwells in darkness
    of Africa,
And thou art fall'n to give me life in regions of dark
    death.' "

Blake will make many allusions to this important event, the beginning of the reconstitution
of Unity, and leave no detail of it unexplained.
He tells us plainly that Orc is Luvah (p. 493).
The *shadowy female* remains longer unexplained,
but her name is also given (p. 394) and the
demons of the deep sing of the nuptials: Then
Orc disappears and Luvah reappears in his
stead:

"So sung the demons of the deep; the Clarions of
    war blew loud.
Orc rent her, and his human form consum'd in his
    own fires
Mingled with her dolorous members strewn thro'
    the Abyss.

[180]

She joy'd in all the Conflict, Gratified and drinking
 tears of woe.
No more remain'd of Orc but the Serpent round the
 tree of Mystery.
The form of Orc was gone;"[1]

That is why the first epic of Blake is called *Vala*:
it is built round this nuptial incident.

This being achieved (namely Passion having
been satisfied), Los can proceed to rebuild
Unity: Imagination, in Art, reconstitutes the
proper mentality of mankind. This is the
building of Golgonooza, the return of the
nations to England, which is the subject of
Jerusalem.[2]

The next step is the regeneration of Urizen.
This is effected by the fact that Los submits
to him (p. 380): the allegory is simple enough:
Imagination, having regenerated Passion (Los
it is that gives Vala to Luvah, p. 379), submits
both Passion and itself to Reason, who is thus
regenerated by admitting within itself both
Imagination and Passion.

Then Urizen is reunited to Ahania, since he

---

[1] P. 394, cf. 217, 255, 345, 371, 376, 379, 391, 394, 401, 408, 413,
427, 493.

[2] Cf. 335, 376, 378, with the plough and the wine-press and similar
metaphors 514-516, 518, 662, and language 624; all this brings
little that is new into the myth.

[181]

has subdued his Spectre, and Tharmas's reunion to Enion follows as a matter of course in
the last book of *Vala*. Golgonooza is built,
Albion awakes and is received by the Immortals
and that is the last book of *Jerusalem*.

Milton remains: *Milton* seems to me a largely
autobiographical poem on Blake's part. Fel-
pham plays in it an altogether disproportionate
part. Blake seems to be bent on explaining his
own mission. He therefore goes into the details
of the crisis relating to Orc and Vala. He tells
us that the first-fruit of that reunion was a
rebirth of Urizen as Satan, the Total Spectre.
That at the same time Luvah was reborn as
Jesus, since mankind is to be saved by Passion
freed and regenerated. So that Luvah was
really divided into two parts:

amalgamated with Urizen he became Satan reborn
of Orc;
as Orc-Luvah, he became Jesus.

One part of Luvah, Jesus, offered itself in
sacrifice for the other part, Satan. Thus Jesus
disappeared in the Sacrifice: Mankind was
saved, no doubt, but Satan-Urizen was still at
large.

This is where Blake comes in: Milton descended

from Heaven, identified himself with Blake, and in this form fought and subdued Urizen. Thus the world was finally saved by Blake's promulgation of the Gospel of Imagination.[1]

This personal intervention of Blake and the circumstances leading to it certainly complicate the myth; but Blake has wisely confined that set of personal complications to the poem entitled *Milton*, which it is therefore best to tackle when the other Prophecies have been mastered.

If we rise from this turmoil of myths to the metaphysical plane, we find that the Reconstitution of the One means chiefly the suppression of the Individual self, which is to be merged into the One Eternal Being.

"Time was Finished! The Breath Divine Breathed
    over Albion
Beneath the Furnaces and starry Wheels and in the
    Immortal Tomb,
And England, who is Brittania, awoke from Death
    on Albion's bosom:
She awoke pale and cold; she fainted seven times on
    the Body of Albion."

. . . .

[1]Orc as Satan: 394-401, 408, 413. Jesus as Luvah: 401-408, 669, Orc-Luvah divided into Jesus + Satan: 414. Satan as Spectre: 552. 598-599; of Albion: 528-529, 540. Satan as Urizen reborn of Orc: 480.

"Compelling Urizen to his Furrow and Tharmas to
his Sheepfold
And Luvah to his Loom. Urthona he beheld, mighty
labouring at
His Anvil, in the Great Spectre Los unwearied
labouring and weeping:
Therefore the Sons of Eden praise Urthona's Spectre
in songs,
Because he kept the Divine Vision in time of trouble."

. . . .

"So spake the Vision of Albion, and in him so
spake in my hearing
The Universal Father. Then Albion stretch'd his
hand into Infinitude
And took his Bow. Fourfold the Vision; for bright
beaming Urizen
Lay'd his hand on the South and took a breathing
Bow of carved Gold:
Luvah his hand stretch'd to the East and bore a
Silver Bow, bright shining:
Tharmas Westward a Bow of Brass, pure flaming,
richly wrought:
Urthona Northward in thick storms a Bow of Iron,
terrible thundering."

. . . .

"All Human Forms identified, even Tree, Metal,
Earth and Stone: all
Human Forms identified, living, going forth and
returning wearied

[184]

99
All Human Forms identified even Tree Metal Earth & Stone. all
Human Forms identified, living going forth & returning wearied
Into the Planetary lives of Years Months Days & Hours reposing
And then Awaking into his Bosom in the Life of Immortality.
And I heard the Name of their Emanations they are named Jerusalem
The End of The Song
of Jerusalem

Albion and Jerusalem re-united

(*Jerusalem*, p. 99)

Into the Planetary lives of Years, Months, Days and
    Hours; reposing,
And then Awaking into his Bosom in the Life of
    Immortality."[1]

The Eternals have helped (665-676) Love on
Earth and collaboration has been established
(379, 385, 516, 518). Urizen has been reconciled
(429) and the work has largely fallen to him,
for Los's building of Art was only a starting
point; but all have joined in (458, 460, 437).
Luvah has made himself a servant (438-457).
Even as the Schekhina is united to God in the
Cabala, Jerusalem has been united to Albion:

"He found Jerusalem upon the River of his City,
    soft repos'd
In the arms of Vala, assimilating in one with Vala,
The Lilly of Havilah; and they sang soft thro'
    Lambeth's vales
In a sweet moony night and silence that they had
    created
With a blue sky spread over with wings and a mild
    moon,
Dividing and uniting into many female forms,
    Jerusalem
Trembling; then in one comingling in eternal tears,
Sighing to melt his Giant beauty on the moony river."[2]

Thus Sex at last is suppressed:

[1] *Jerusalem*, pp. 743-751.   [2] P. 585.

"In Eternity they neither marry nor are given in marriage."[1]

Even as Los had told Enitharmon:

"Los answer'd swift as the shuttle of gold: 'Sexes must vanish and cease
To be when Albion arises from his dread repose, O lovely Enitharmon:
When all their Crimes, their Punishments, their Accusations of Sin,
All their Jealousies, Revenges, Murders, hidings of Cruelty in Deceit
Appear only in the Outward Spheres of Visionary Space and Time,
In the shadows of Possibility, by Mutual Forgiveness for evermore,
And in the Vision and in the Prophecy, that we may Foresee and Avoid
The terrors of Creation and Redemption and Judgment."[2]

Thus the Zoas having united, the Sexes having disappeared by union, the Self disappears:

"Albion reply'd: 'Cannot Man exist without Mysterious
Offering of Self for Another? is this Friendship and Brotherhood?
I see thee in the likeness and similitude of Los my Friend.'

[1]P. 614.   [2]Pp. 739-740.

Jesus said: 'Wouldest thou love one who never died
For thee, or ever die for one who had not died for
    thee?
And if God dieth not for Man and giveth not himself
Eternally for Man, Man could not exist; for Man is
    Love
As God is Love: every kindness to another is a little
    Death
In the Divine Image, nor can Man exist but by
    Brotherhood.'

So saying the Cloud overshadowing divided them
    asunder.
Albion stood in terror, not for himself but for his
    Friend
Divine; and Self was lost in the contemplation of
    faith
And wonder at the Divine Mercy and at Los's
    sublime honour."[1]

.   .   .   .

"To open the Eternal Worlds, to open the immortal
    Eyes
Of Man inwards into the Worlds of Thought, into
    Eternity
Ever expanding in the Bosom of God, the Human
    Imagination.
O Saviour pour upon me thy Spirit of meekness and
    love!
Annihilate the Selfhood in me: be thou all my life!"[2]

.   .   .   .

[1]P. 746.   [2]P. 554.

"Los cries: 'No Individual ought to appropriate to
   Himself
Or to his Emanation any of the Universal Charac-
   teristics
Of David or of Eve, of the Woman or of the Lord,
Of Reuben or of Benjamin, of Joseph or Judah or
   Levi.
Those who dare appropriate to themselves Universal
   Attributes
Are the Blasphemous Selfhoods, and must be broken
   asunder."[1]

Milton says to Satan:

                    ". . . I come to Self Annihilation.
Such are the Laws of Eternity, that each shall
   mutually
Annihilate himself for others' good, as I for thee.
Thy purpose and the purpose of thy Priests and of
   thy Churches
Is to impress on men the fear of death, to teach
Trembling and fear, terror, constriction, abject
   selfishness.
Mine is to teach Men to despise death and to
   go on
In fearless majesty annihilating Self, laughing to
   scorn
Thy Laws and terrors, shaking down thy Synagogues
   as webs."

·   ·   ·   ·   ·   ·   ·   ·   ·   ·

[1]P. 734.

"In Self annihilation all that is not of God alone,
To put off Self and all I have, ever and ever. Amen."[1]

In sober prose, Blake is even more explicit.

"Many suppose that before the Creation All was
Solitude and Chaos. This is the most pernicious
Idea that can enter the Mind, as it takes away all
sublimity from the Bible and Limits All Existence
to Creation and to Chaos, To the Time and Space
fixed by the Corporeal Vegetative Eye, and leaves
the Man who entertains such an Idea the habitation
of Unbelieving demons. Eternity Exists, and All
things in Eternity, Independent of Creation which
was an act of Mercy. I have represented those who
are in Eternity by some in a Cloud within the Rain-
bow that Surrounds the Throne; they merely appear
as in a Cloud when any thing of Creation, Redemption or Judgement are the Subjects of Contemplation,
tho' their Whole Contemplation is concerning these
things; the Reason they so appear is The Humiliation
of the Reason and doubting Selfhood, and the Giving
all up to Inspiration. By this it will be seen that I
do not consider either the Just or the Wicked to be
in a Supreme State, but to be every one of them
States of the Sleep which the Soul may fall into in
its deadly dreams of Good and Evil when it leaves
Paradise following the Serpent."[2]

The individual soul has no reality left—not

[1]Pp. 541, 542.   [2]Pp. 840-841.

even moral merit or demerit. Blake has passed beyond good and evil; he has passed beyond the self. He believes only in the One Eternal Soul as a lasting entity, as a reality into which we are to awake from our fleeting, individual dreams.

CONCLUSION

I T appears thus that Blake's ideas, considered as a whole, are perfectly coherent and reasonable.

He has expressed with great power the chief conceptions of his age and therefore of ours. He has remoulded with a very impressive force of imagination the myths he has taken from the Cabala, from India, from the Gnostics and from still other sources very probably.

His most original contribution to the body of thought he has given expression to is, it seems to me, his transformation of the old moral meaning of *Self Annihilation*. Blake has seen in man not so much an undividable entity, as a congregation of states[1]: gathered together in him, they appear as one being. Behind them is only the One; there is only one being in the

---

[1]And yet it must be pointed out that Hume had seen in the self only "a bundle of perceptions." (*Treatise on Human Nature*, 1739, i., iv., quoted by Windeband, p. 474 of Tuft's translation of the *History of Philosophy*.) Blake's idea is quite different from Hume's and the self is for Blake rather a bundle of moods. Hume's conceptions are very distant from Blake's but Blake, with his time, is heir to Hume's criticism of experience and intellect.

world. This is an old conception, which may have come to Blake from Plotinus or from India, whatever the ways by which it came. But in his ingenious application of it to the theory of States, of the Mighty ones in every man, Blake appears to me to have been thinking in advance of his age; though not necessarily always thinking rightly.

A forerunner of Nietzsche by his subversion of moral values, he is also a forerunner of Proust by this theory of states as more permanent than individuals: which means that his intellectual force is not yet spent.

In some ways his poetical imagination enabled him to go further than our great contemporaries. For there is in poetical genius an innate balance and power of synthesis which is often absent from more prosaic minds.

Thus, Blake, while he upset the ordinary laws of morality much in the same manner as Nietzsche (Was Jesus gentle?—) yet kept an underlying principle of love to all and a sense of the value of all beings. Nietzsche, in his noble cruelty, tried to do away with degraded beings. Man is something that must be surpassed and destroyed. But to Blake, however degraded, all beings are in some way, part of the One. The Nietzschean division between aristocrat and mob with a different morality for each, is not in Blake. Blake's division between the good and the evil is not of the same kind: Blake acknowledges the necessity of the "good," even if he wants to be "evil" and he will regenerate every one.

Thus there is more synthesis in Blake than in Nietzsche, who divides more than he unites. Also there is more real common sense in Blake: Blake keeps the essence of Christian beliefs, which Nietzsche really does not understand, and the underlying modes of thought of both Old and New Testaments are the common sense of the Western World. Blake is thus less paradoxical than Nietzsche. For instance, on the question of woman: there is a great distance between Blake's conception of the necessity of woman to man, his picture of the state of man without woman, and Nietzsche's disdainful but insufficient conception of woman as the amusement of the warrior. Perhaps this is not· quite fair to Nietzsche, but I believe the fact remains that disciples of Nietzsche can go to Blake and learn.

And so can, perhaps, disciples of Proust.

If we interpret Proust in Blakean terms, we can

[193]

say that for Proust the only permanent thing in us is The Eternal Man. He appears in us now and then, here and there, when Marcel is sipping his tea or catching a glimpse of two spires in the distance or listening to Vinteuil's music; He appears in us in the moments of ecstasy. Then we have the feeling that we are transported beyond time and cease to care whether we are mortal or not.[1]

These moments would be to Blake the moments when the four elements are reconciled, and the Eternal Man is realised, as during inspiration.

For Proust, separate states are more lasting than individuals. Thus the elements fighting in us (as in the admirable description of the grandmother's death) in the mineral world, are states in us dating from the beginning of the world. It might be Tharmas fighting Luvah. Thus a light little state of mirth expressed in a peculiar sort of laughter has been for centuries running about the courts of Southern Germany and has lasted on into our friend, Robert de Saint Soup. The individuals in whom it lived have disappeared, but it remains. Even so, Blake's states are permanent where the

[1] See D. Saurat: *Tendances* (Monde Moderne, Paris), where the Proustian texts bearing on this question are collected.

individuals, made up by passing conjunctions of the Zoas, are transitory.

Yet Proust gives the individual a chance to survive, at least partly, as the famous passage on the death of Bergotte shows clearly. Perhaps our present tendency (in spite of many appearances) is to insist more and more on the value of personality in the individual as against the nineteenth century's tendency to belittle and disperse personality. Let us note in connection with this that Blake keeps a personal god and insists, in his peculiar manner, that one cannot love a cloud though one can love an old man in the cloud. But we can go deeper than that. Blake's conception of Unity is complex. Urizen and Los and Tharmas and Luvah are not suppressed and melted into one, but harmonised. They are made into a whole in which each remains an individual:

—And they conversed together in visionary forms dramatic—

Nor do the Zoa and his emanation merge into One: in order to enjoy their union they must remain twain. They are reunited, not melted, into one. This is in line with Cabalistic thinking: It is in order to enjoy the relationship that God separates the Matrona from himself and creates individual beings within himself.

When we cease to be "just" or "wicked," we shall not be entirely suppressed, only remoulded; some of our states will be cast out everlastingly; but judging by what happens to Blake's Zoas, we may hope that the better part of us will remain as an individual within the One Individual, God, much as a limb of ours, has in a sense separate identity and feeling within our total being.

In this Blake again goes much further than Proust: his mythology helps him to a synthesis, where the purely analytical mind of the great French novelist sees only the vaguest symptoms of a synthesis. Here lies the justification of Blake's mythology, for which we thus have to be grateful, however impatient it may have made us feel at times.

Another curious trait they have in common is the importance played by the feeling of jealousy in both their worlds. Jealousy is the chief active feeling with Proust. Much more active than love. Marcel can really only be in love when in the state of jealousy; this feeling makes him decide to marry, or rather to sequestrate Albertine, is the chief mover of *Un Amour de*

Swann, of *La Prisonnière* and a good half of *Albertine Disparue.* Thus Proust has cabalistic connotations: Proust's theory of love is that love is the acute feeling that we need another being to have a complete life; that, separately, we are only half a being. And this, as we have seen, is the cabalistic conception parallel to Blake's myth of emanation and spectre. Hence in Proust the horror that comes over us when we feel this indispensable half escaping from our possession; Blake knows of this horror, which is that felt by Theotormon,

Upon the margin'd ocean, conversing with shadows
    dire.

(A wonderful epic description, far beyond Proust's power, of Marcel's feelings relating to Albertine and the sea.)
Blake disapproved of this jealousy in theory (in practice, he is supposed to have yielded to his wife's jealousy), but that theory applies only to this world: in the world of Unity, each emanation is given back to her Zoa. Jealousy ceases, it is true, but it is because each being is united to the One he loves, and all the pieces of the puzzle are fitted each into their proper place. In this world, for Blake as for Proust,

jealousy reigns, and Urizen is called *Father of Jealousy.*

Let us insist again that Proust merely notes the fact, whereas Blake notes and passes judgment. Moral judgment is of no value, as Proust would not admit of it. But Blake passes judgment metaphysically in the name of the Divine Unity. Proust, of course, cannot follow. Here again Blake achieves a synthesis where our contemporary attains only analysis.

This will be our conclusion. Blake's peculiar usefulness in our time is in his power of synthesis, or at least in his desire for synthesis. He blends together perhaps more elements than any other modern writer. And when reason cannot blend them, he flies off into mythology. Thus, at least, he makes the problem tangible, in a way, and gives an indication of the direction in which he would seek a solution.

In the human spirit, he attempts a synthesis of reason, imagination, passion and instinct. Let us mention, to make clear the magnitude of the attempt, that Milton was concerned fundamentally only with two, reason and passion, and that most writers of the romantic school, from Byron to Verlaine, rarely grasped more

[198]

than one of these states, generally not reason;
that Victor Hugo, intellectually the most
advanced of Blake's successors, could only
bring three into his synthesis, namely, reason,
imagination and instinct.[1]

In the history of the human mind, Blake keeps
the best of Christianity in the spirit of love and
forgiveness; and the best of the rationalist
revolt against Christianity in the spirit of
relentless intellectual criticism and sincerity.
He attempted to blend the passion of the
religious seeker and the instinctive optimism of
mankind with the wildest imagination of the
artist and yet the coolness and the solidity of
reason. Is it a wonder that he often failed?

His fault was that he attempted too much. His
synthesis was planned on too grand a scale,
and not achieved. But the elements of the
synthesis are all there, for the successive
generations to try again, by the lesson of his
failure. For in conveying the spirit of his enter-
prise he did not fail; much more than in this
or that idea, however deep, we find Blake's
lesson in the inimitable sweetness and peculiar
mode of his song: a unique mingling of gentle-

[1]See on this, D. Saurat: *La Religion de Victor Hugo* (Introduction),
Paris, 1929.

ness and audacity, of power and of phantasy; hard as Urizen, hopeful as Los, passionate as Luvah, warm and universal as Tharmas.

That synthesis which is impossible to philosophy, Blake has, occasionally, achieved it in poetry. Hence his greatness, and his permanent value.